IMPACT
Without
Authority

Other Books From SAMA

Harnessing Global Potential: Insights Into Managing Customers Worldwide
By Kevin Wilson, Tony Millman, Dan Weilbaker and Simon Croom

The Trust Imperative: The Competitive Advantage of Trust-Based Business Relationships
By Roger Dow, Lisa Napolitano and Mike Pusateri

Unlocking Profits: The Strategic Advantage of Key Account Management
By Ginger Conlon, Lisa Napolitano and Mike Pusateri

For more information about these books call, fax or write:

SAMA
150 N. Wacker Dr., Suite 2222
Chicago, IL 60606

Tel: 312-251-3131
Fax: 312-251-3132

E-mail: sales@strategicaccounts.org
Website: www.strategicaccounts.org

IMPACT
Without
Authority

How to Leverage Internal Resources to Create Customer Value

By:

Jane Helsing
Vice President, Strategic Accounts
Personnel Decisions International

Barbara Geraghty
President
Visionary Selling

Lisa Napolitano
President & CEO
Strategic Account Management Association

S A M A

Strategic Account Management Association
150 North Wacker Drive, Suite 2222
Chicago, Illinois 60606

Designed by Aimee Waddell
Copy Editing by Melissa Olson
Manufactured in the United States of America

Library of Congress Cataloging-in-Publication Data

Helsing, Jane
  Impact Without Authority: How to Leverage Internal Resources to Create
Customer Value / Jane Helsing, Barbara Geraghty, Lisa Napolitano

ISBN 0-9728836-90-X $19.95

To Our Parents,

For teaching us the power of a full heart,

a curious mind and a positive attitude.

Contents

Preface

"An ounce of action is worth a ton of theory."
Friedrich Engels
German Social Philosopher, 1820-1895

Why Write This Book?
Because You've Got to Start Somewhere...

Although the decision to write this book was made in the spring of 2002, the seed was planted several years earlier at a SAMA Annual Conference networking reception. The setting was social and the mood was relaxed, but the conversation was nevertheless centered on the issues keeping this experienced group of strategic sales executives awake at night. Typical of that time, everyone was talking about their challenges in dealing with their customers. Effectively navigating the customer organization, particularly in pursuit of a dialogue with non-procurement senior executives, was the burning issue of the day. The group nodded and gestured enthusiastically as the war stories were shared, until someone brought the conversation to a screeching halt with this statement:

*"My customers <u>love</u> me...it's my own organization
that treats me like the enemy!"*

And right there amidst the façade of a desert oasis began the paradigm shift.

Perhaps that's why the comment still sticks in my mind...it was truly an inverted perspective that would soon become the most pervasive, talked about issue I have encountered since I began with SAMA in 1991. I honestly don't remember what happened next in this scenario. My guess is that we either moved on to some other, more familiar topic, or just adjourned to the nearest pool table. What

I do know is that I filed away that comment, and it gnawed at me over time as the global business environment continued to undergo dramatic transformation.

Over time, the buzz around "internal issues" started to grow, although "selling to the executive level" and "understanding your customer's business better than they do" were the typical hot topics. Then, seemingly overnight, the firms with the very best SAM practices (against whom the rest had been benchmarking) started experiencing greater difficulty in maintaining their program momentum. Some even scaled back or disbanded their programs in the face of short-term diminishing returns on their investment in SAM. Highly skilled and experienced account managers started having greater difficulty meeting their objectives. And then the complaints started to mount, only *this* time, they weren't complaining about their customers:

> *My main challenge is internal inertia...my customers are much more willing to form alliances than my own company.*

> *I've got to find ways for my company to act as a whole when dealing with our national accounts, not as individual units.*

> *How do you get buy-in from a traditional transactional-based sales force that has been explained the role of strategic accounts (beyond price and product) but refuses to understand its importance? Help!*

> *How does the SAM instill in its company the same sense of urgency to meet the customer's need that the strategic account executive himself brings from the customer meeting?*

> *It's a lack of priority, a lack of global alignment, a lack of trust, a lack of communication, a lack of empathy, a lack of support systems...lack, lack, lack, lack! And those get magnified as you add culture and language and time zones and other stuff.*

Because SAMA's hallmark is facilitating the sharing of best practices, we began to search for remedies to what was obviously a serious, and growing, problem. The trouble was that we ran into a brick wall. The companies with established programs, serious investment and solid commitment didn't have much in the way of a solution to the "internal issues"—they were struggling with them as well! And ticking off the checklist of *Critical Success Factors for Strategic Account Management* that was accepted at the time didn't explain why firms who had those elements in place weren't faring any better. What was going on?

My working theory is that two major shifts were occurring

simultaneously that, in tandem, brought the inefficiencies of today's business processes and structures into sharp focus:

1. Customers were getting smarter about managing their supply chain to not only leverage the growth period, but to survive the effects consolidation was having on their market position. This revolution was driving suppliers to change, with the pressure to do so rapidly increasing as customers got more savvy, more sizeable and more desperate to find efficiencies in the face of a shrinking economy.

AT THE SAME TIME...

2. Sales organizations, almost exclusively externally focused by nature, were paralyzed by a new set of customer expectations that required an enterprise response. In their attempt to successfully mobilize their firm's resources and people, SAMs and SAM Program Managers ran head first into a wide range of obstacles including apathy, contending priorities and even active resistance. All the work trying to penetrate the customer to identify sources of new value was fruitless if the supplier couldn't – or wouldn't – deliver on it. And firms just weren't prepared for the organizational challenge of creating alignment that extended to the far reaches of every silo.

Clearly, the people experiencing the most pain amidst this sea change were members of the corporate sales team. Not only were they feeling the pressure of decreasing sales and dwindling margins, they had insufficient authority to do anything significant about it. The customer was losing; the supplier was losing; and smack in the middle stood the SAM team.

This book is an attempt to start to change all that. Until now, much of the dialogue has focused on *describing* the many varieties of internal problems, culminating in a call to action to fix them. When we looked at what was available in the way of HOW to fix them, we found that while the tools to help SAMs sell to customers have increased in number and sophistication, there simply weren't many out there to help SAMs sell internally. There was no denying that SAMA needed not only to examine these challenges in a way relevant to SAM practitioners, but to provide a set of practical tools to help build individual skills and organizational competencies to combat them.

SAMA has partnered with true thought leaders to bring together the content of this book. Both Jane Helsing and Barbara Geraghty bring to this subject not only a long, successful career in sales, but also a "post-sales" wealth of experience developing tools and processes to help sales organizations succeed in this ever-changing business environment. Backed by the cutting edge content of Personnel Decisions International (PDI) and Visionary Selling, SAMA is privileged to have worked with such knowledgeable contributors. In addition, the book is filled with the wisdom and experience of peers such as yourself—some who will share with you the successes they have achieved, and some who provide a familiar voice as they articulate their ongoing struggles.

What You Will Learn

Although this book is primarily written for the individuals at the customer interface, it contains specific messages aimed toward the various decision-makers in your firm responsible for setting broad strategy and policy. Reading this book will provide a "roadmap" to follow as you establish your ability to impact the areas of your organization that touch the customer—regardless of your level of authority.

Part I describes the issue in the context of our current business environment and sets forth a mandate for change to begin to resolve it. **Part II** outlines a six-step process to increase your ability to effectively navigate your own company and marshal resources on behalf of the customer. **Part III** explains how senior management can help remove obstacles to customer focus and develop organizational competencies for sustained success.

If you are a SAM, you will learn:

- How to represent your customers and leverage internal resources to achieve customer value;
- How to sell your ideas and get your voice heard within your company;
- How to obtain executive buy-in and support;
- How top salespeople sell internally; and
- How to create alignment through win-win solutions.

If you are in Management, you will learn:

- What you can do to create organizational support for SAMs;
- How your contributions will translate into increased success;
- How to take ownership and lead change; and
- How to make customer focus a genuine executive suite priority.

If you are a CEO, you will learn:

- What SAMs are facing as they try to deliver innovative solutions to your company's most important accounts;

- How corporate decisions are negatively impacting your sales performance;

- What your company risks by not addressing the internal conflict caused by silos; and

- How to become the Chief Customer Officer leading the charge for customer advocacy throughout your entire organization.

The Outcome We Hope For

"You can either take action, or you can hang back and hope for a miracle. Miracles are great, but they are so unpredictable."

Peter F. Drucker

By now you may have noticed that I haven't said much about "Authority". That's because there's not much to say about it except to acknowledge that what little of it is actually parceled out in today's complex corporation is never far-reaching enough to cover the vast number of people that a customer advocate needs to influence. Don't get me wrong—Authority *is* an issue dealt with in this book, but primarily in the context of determining who DOES have authority and what you must do to get them to make decisions that are in line with your key customer strategies. To dwell too much on the authority you don't have is a recipe for paralysis. To blame current ineffectiveness on the absence of more authority is to ignore your true role as internal advocate on behalf of your customer. Or in the words of one SAMA member:

"We should exist to serve our customer, and getting shot at in the crossfire probably isn't the most productive thing to do all the time."

Lisa Napolitano
President & CEO
Strategic Account Management Association
April, 2003

Acknowledgements

From Jane –

First, I never would have been able to write this book without the support and help throughout my career that I've received from my husband, Bryan Eichenwald. He is a source of strength and encouragement for me.

I also want to acknowledge the wonderful backing on this project provided by my boss, Joanne Provo; my sponsor for this project, Sue Gebelein; and PDI in general. My own work group was most affected by my taking the time to work on this book, so I thank them all for their patience. Several of my co-workers provided collaboration and content, including David Armstrong, Eric Engwall, Gary Gerds, Terry Gray, Kristi Hommerding, Bill Johnston, Bridget Lane, Donna Neumann and Kathy Schoenbauer.

Other PDI teammembers whose expertise is woven throughout these pages include David Peterson, who authored Chapter 7; Lucy Dahl (now at Dell Computer), Cori Hill, Max Lazovick, Kristie Nelson-Neuhaus, Sandra Allen O'Connor, Lou Quast, Carol Skube, Elaine Sloan, Marc Sokol, Jeff Stoner and Linda Van Den Boom.

And I would be remiss if I did not also acknowledge the role my clients have played in my own development. Although my role is to impart skills and knowledge, I learn so very much from you. Thank you!

From Lisa –

I need to first thank the SAMA staff for pulling out all the stops to make yet another one of my ridiculous project deadlines. The next time you roll your eyes at my timeline, I promise not to get angry. If you roll your eyes at my IDEA, then all bets are off. In particular, I need to recognize Aimee Waddell and Peg Kelly for their fabulous design and dedication to quality, Melissa Olson for her great editing and overall patience in helping to manage this project, and Maria Susano for cleaning up after my mess yet again and rarely disliking anything I write.

Thank you to SAMA's Board of Director's which has always allowed me a great deal of freedom in my role on behalf of the organization, especially given my tendency to ask for forgiveness as opposed to permission. It has been a privilege to learn from and work beside you and all the people in the SAMA Network. I challenge you to find an adult anywhere who loves his or her job more than I do.

Finally, I'd like to thank my family for raising me in an environment where discourse is a contact sport. Although this book will probably end up propping open a door somewhere, you'll give me a hell of an argument about the concepts without having even read it. GOD, I love you guys!

PART I
The Issue

Part I:
The Issue

"The number of people in the organization working on the relationship with the customer, relative to the total organization, will determine the momentum of the organization."

Bob Buckman, CEO, Buckman Labs

Your customers are your future, and your most strategic customers come first. Their success or failure will have a critical impact on your company, which makes *their* business *your* business. In fact, their strategy should be driving your strategy, not the other way around. Just what *is* their strategy? Marketplace winners don't just buy products and services—they buy expectations. Superior product and flawless performance is taken for granted...it is merely the price of entry into the game. What strategic customers want is the commitment of and access to the supplier's total operation. They want problem solving and creative thinking about their business. Your company's ability to deliver on these expectations is largely dependent upon the level of commitment your entire company has to your strategic account management program. But even strong commitment to the strategy isn't enough to be successful anymore. It takes the efforts of an entire organization to enable a supplier to deliver customer value, and the task of aligning all its various components is huge. It is also difficult, painful, expensive and frustrating, but the one thing it's **NOT** is optional. Effective strategic customer management is about investing in building relationships with customers who are future marketplace winners. Failure to do so will leave you in the company of the losers, which is a recipe for disaster that may not manifest itself until it is too late to recover.

It's tempting to jump right into problem-solving mode because, frankly, there's too much to do and too little time. Besides, few sales practitioners lack awareness of "What" is going on that is derailing

Part I: The Issue

3

their efforts to deliver value to customers. The danger here is that your perception of what is going on may not be as accurate as you think. You are not alone in your internal struggles, and there are concrete reasons for that. There are universal drivers behind these current business challenges that merit consideration. Taking a closer look at the "Why" behind the "What" is likely to provide you with fresh insights into "How" you should tackle these challenges. That said, when it's time to turn your focus inward on your own company's issues, there is still much diagnosing to be done. Despite the overwhelming parallels between corporations trying to be more customer-focused, the fact remains that understanding the unique details of how they come into play inside your firm is critical to formulating an effective plan of action. **PART I** of this book is designed to help you see the big picture with even greater clarity. Use it to stretch your thinking and challenge your current framework regarding these issues. Then use it to help you make the broader business case for change inside your company.

Chapter 1 platforms the realities of today's marketplace and illustrates the forces at work that are changing our way of interacting in the business environment. Starting with the customer – as we always must – this chapter explores the true nature of the difficulties in meeting customer expectations and describes the paradigm shift required by suppliers to rise to the challenge. We'll investigate the enormous gap between embracing a strategy for customer-focus and actually executing on it. And, finally, we'll tackle the challenge of internal alignment, identifying the inherent barriers that exist and outlining the enablers of a collaborative culture inside your firm.

In **Chapter 2**, we launch into problem-solving mode, starting with an inventory of what needs to change inside your firm and ways to bring it about in a broader sense. Because the scope of effort required is far-reaching, we'll identify the various internal players responsible for driving customer-focus and outline their role in this undertaking. Included in this discussion will be ideas for how you, as an individual, can disseminate these messages across your organization to spark change, foster enthusiasm and create momentum. Finally, we will begin our focus on you, the reader, and what you need to do to have greater IMPACT within your own company in order to have greater IMPACT on your customer.

By the end of **PART I**, we hope to have imparted some new ideas and fresh perspectives on the challenges you face. We believe this important foundation will best prepare you to leverage **PART II**, which will provide you with the tools to start having greater IMPACT now.

Chapter 1:
What Customers Want and Why It's So Difficult to Deliver

"So, apart from the fact that we're not price competitive, we're inconsistent, inflexible, unresponsive and arrogant—are there any other barriers to our doing more business together?"

In the midst of rampant consolidation and rapid globalization, customers are demanding far more from their suppliers than ever before as they rethink their business strategies to provide higher shareholder returns. A key component of their strategy is to develop a laser beam focus on what they are really good at – their "core competencies" – and outsource the rest to those who can do it better. Recognizing that the bandwidth for true value-based business partnerships is rather narrow, customers are also sizing up suppliers in terms of which ones can help further their strategies, and rearranging their internal processes to focus more on those relationships and much less on all the others. By concentrating their business with a smaller number of supplier firms, customers hope to achieve higher degrees of control over their providers, greater accountability for results, transparency in financial terms and greater convenience that comes from having to deal with fewer providers, all of whom know the client intimately.

Core suppler criteria now include:

- The ability to impact the overall performance of the customer's business across a range of products and geography;

- The ability of a supplier to survive in a consolidating industry. There is an opportunity cost to granting core relationship status to a supplier that is unlikely to have a long-term future;

- The ability to invest in developing a unique set of services for the customer;

- The likelihood that the customer will be of strategic importance to the supplier, rather than merely receiving opportunistic service and coverage;

- The ability of the supplier to make a sustained commitment to market leadership in specific products and markets; and

- The ability to consistently deliver on the promise of integrated service across the supplier's organization.

This new reality requires a realization by suppliers that <u>your customers are your future</u>.

 "The value of a firm is ultimately equal to the sum of the values of its customer relationships. By viewing itself as managing a portfolio of customer relationships, a firm can maximize its value by effectively deploying its customer acquisition, development and retention resources. You cannot develop a customer-based strategy simply by bolting new customer service, satisfaction or loyalty programs onto a vehicle propelled by product-driven thinking."

As customers make these choices, they are, in effect, determining your strategy, and there will be winners and losers as a consequence of those decisions. Effective strategic customer management is proactive, not reactive. The customers who gain market share will take their core suppliers with them as they prosper. If you are slow to align yourself with the future winners, not only will you not enjoy the fruits of their success, you will be left in the company of the marketplace losers. By the way, revenue and profit won't be the only items left on the table. Successful companies breed innovation with whomever they spend their quality time. If your competition gets the cash, the profit AND the best ideas, that doesn't bode well for your firm's future.

Many firms not previously committed to the concept of strategic customer management have responded to these market realities by reconsidering the strategy, often with a keen sense of urgency because a competitor or two had bought in to it years before. Firms with existing programs tend to fall into two extreme camps depending on their prior successes in strategic account management. Those who have seen an ROI in the past and have a substantive structure to support key activities have continued to invest in SAM to keep up with the growing business requirements of their most important customers. Those who have struggled to make it work and have little evidence of the financial benefits of this expensive strategy have either stalled or disbanded their efforts in the face of growing pressure to cut costs.

Remember, it is an entirely appropriate strategic choice to eschew customer-supplier partnering in favor of being the low-cost provider, as long as your infrastructure is in line with that strategy. The danger is for those firms who choose a value-based posture in word but cannot deliver that value in deed, thereby supporting a costly coverage model only to be viewed by customers as a commodity vendor. Even the most sophisticated, experienced, entrenched SAM programs are struggling to build an integrated view of the total customer relationship across products and geographies. Simply put, leveraging your position around the world as one unit is an enormous challenge under even the most favorable circumstances.

The Broad Execution Challenge: A Question of Alignment

"Most often today the difference between a company and its competitor is the ability to execute. If your competitors are executing better than you are, they're beating you in the here and now, and the financial markets won't wait to see if your elaborate strategy plays out. Execution is the great unaddressed issue in the business world today. Its absence is the single biggest obstacle to success and the cause of most of the disappointments that are mistakenly attributed to other causes."

Ram Charan, author of
Execution: The Discipline of Getting Things Done

The latest management thinking has taken a sharp turn away from the past several decades of strategy obsession and landed squarely on the issue of execution. In his recent bestseller on the issue of execution, management guru Ram Charan recalls noticing the problem of execution more than three decades ago, as he repeatedly observed that strategic plans often did not work out in practice. "As I facilitated meetings at the CEO and division levels," writes Charan, "I watched and studied, and I saw that leaders placed too much emphasis on what some call high-level strategy, on intellectualizing and philosophizing and not enough on implementation. People would agree on a project or initiative, and then nothing would come of it. In time I saw a pattern and realized that execution was a major issue." According to Charan, the fundamental problem is that strategy is perceived as the important work of the firm's best thinkers, while execution is considered to be operational—the tactical side of the business that is relegated to the worker bees. Charan's entire book is devoted to the argument that execution is actually a *discipline* and a *system* that must be built into a company's strategy, its goals and its culture. Without an execution culture, the perfect strategy is nothing more than a dream—some might even argue a nightmare.

It's no surprise, then, that senior executives routinely affirm that it is not the lack of a strategy that causes them to lose sleep, but, rather, their organization's inability to execute against a strategy, often long after they think they have expressed that strategy with near-perfect clarity. Their nervousness is understandable. *Fortune* magazine estimated recently that about 70% of CEO failures are caused not by flawed strategic thinking, but by failure to execute. Moreover, the ability to execute, on its own, is apparently not enough to consistently win. Research has shown that a good plan violently executed right now produces far better results than a perfect plan executed next week.

Why is it so difficult to execute, and what is bringing this issue to the forefront at this point in time? I point you to an excellent article that appeared in the Q4 2000 issue of *Strategy + Business*, "The Organization vs. the Strategy: Solving the Alignment Paradox." The authors argue that many of the execution issues that large firms face are in fact symptoms of dynamic and complex problems embedded in the company's organizational model. For a management consulting piece on such a weighty subject, it's a terrific resource for examining the forces at work in your firm (and your customers' firms) that are contributing to the inefficiencies you're encountering. The condensed message of the piece is that the execution of strategy in today's larger, more complicated organizations requires alignment across a myriad of functional, geographical and product-focused silos. Yet alignment is tough to achieve in an environment where thousands of decisions and trade-offs must be made every day at an individual level, each taking place in a unique setting whereby the individual has access to different information, has different objectives and may face different consequences from his or her actions. Obviously, the majority of these are not the big decisions that get boardroom attention; rather, they are the thousands of daily decisions that are individually small, but collectively huge. It follows logically, then, that competitors with inferior organizational models will continue to suffer from sub-optimal decision-making and will always be a step behind. This may not seem like much, but the authors point out that if you compare it to the difference between a quarterback completing 40% of his passes and 60% of his passes, over time it makes a big impact on the scoreboard.

The Beauty of the Matrix

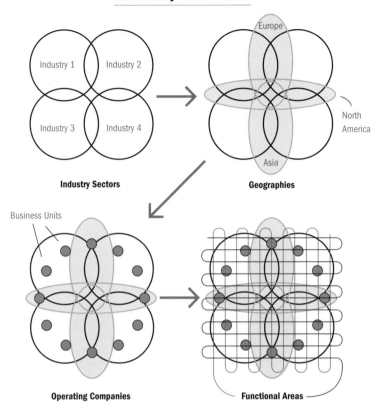

Industry 1 Industry 2
Industry 3 Industry 4
Industry Sectors

Europe
North America
Asia
Geographies

Business Units
Operating Companies

Functional Areas

The answer, however, is not to eradicate the matrix. Corporations of any significant size cannot make all the necessary transactional decisions "with one mind." To provide manageable spans of control and to benefit from functional specialization, companies are forced to subdivide their organizations. Unfortunately, this subdivision fragments the information, decision rights, measures and rewards that guide individual decisions. People's natural tendency is to focus on the more narrowly focused objectives defined by a function or business unit, rather than on company-wide objectives. The resulting divergent views and objectives are what foster organizational silos and drive interdepartmental friction.

> *An organization built on this type of decision-making is incapable of optimizing for the company as a whole.*

If we can't blow up the matrix, then what is to be done? I wish I could tell you the remedy was a simple one. And even though it's not, it's beyond the purview of this book, and most likely, your sphere of influence inside your company. It is, however, an appropriate topic for the most senior decision-makers in your firm to tackle, and one you may wish to explore further for the purposes of bringing some of these concepts to their attention. Our aim in examining this issue here is to highlight the inherent obstacles to alignment in today's predominant organizational models. Key take-aways are:

- The very models that foster misalignment are nevertheless necessary to prevent utter chaos inside a firm;

- To change such models is not impossible, but it is complex and arduous and, therefore, not likely to occur inside your firm any time soon;

- Most firms face the same barriers to alignment that yours does **(good news!)**;

- Incremental improvement in alignment inside your firm is a source of competitive advantage; and

- You as an individual have the potential to incrementally improve alignment in your firm **(good news...read on!)**.

The Challenge of Strategic Account Management Execution

Strategic customer management is, quite possibly, the toughest execution challenge facing companies today. Why? Because the degree of alignment required to bring the collective value of your firm to bear on your customer's business is enormous. It requires the involvement and cooperation of multiple functional areas within both supplier and customer firms. It requires integrating the different stakeholders into a single organization with a common identity and purpose. It requires bringing the voice of the customer into your organization and mobilizing company-wide resources to focus on that voice.

Bottom line—it requires a major paradigm shift inside your company.

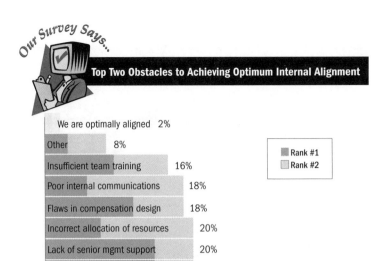

Top Two Obstacles to Achieving Optimum Internal Alignment

We are optimally aligned	2%
Other	8%
Insufficient team training	16%
Poor internal communications	18%
Flaws in compensation design	18%
Incorrect allocation of resources	20%
Lack of senior mgmt support	20%
Insufficient SAM training	20%
Company reporting structure	22%
Lack of buy-in for corporate SAM / GAM	24%
Company culture / Silo mentality	32%

Rank #1
Rank #2

0%   10%   20%   30%   40%

Source: 2001, SAMA Annual Conference Survey of Attendees.

Silo Mentality: Dealing with Turf Battles

According to SAMA research, the single biggest obstacle to alignment is silo mentality revolving around a variety of "turf" issues. Because turf issues can surface in business units, functions or geographies – and in many cases all three simultaneously – they are particularly insidious when trying to present one face to the customer. The root of such conflict usually involves perceptions of incompatible goals or threats to relationships. These perceptions lead to "turf protection" as organizations decide to defend their domain rather than share with another organization. Every time two organizations interact, they establish boundaries through exchange relationships. The basic factor in triggering a turf battle is the degree of power surrendered or gained by the organizations involved. If both organizations feel they will gain by working together or having access to an equal degree of power, cooperation continues. But if one organization feels it has too much to lose by continued cooperation, it begins to defend its turf.

The origins of turf battles are numerous and important to correctly diagnose in order to successfully diffuse them:

- *Resources:* In a climate of shrinking resources, entities often end up competing against one another for a piece of the limited pie. If one organization perceives the "cost" to cooperation in terms of money, time or energy to be greater than the benefits, it will resist it.

- *Goals:* Even if there is consensus on overarching corporate goals, specific joint actions are often perceived to work against the interest of one organization or against another limited goal. The degree to which an entity feels it is flexible to change its current goals, tasks and philosophy to adopt the course of action being proposed will also have an impact.

- *Geography:* To allow another entity to operate in one organization's area is often perceived as an indication that it alone is not doing an adequate job. It also may be perceived as a duplication of effort, or a source of potential confusion to target audiences.

- *Methods:* General agreement on goals alone can still lead to conflict if one party feels the approach proposed to reach goals would be ineffective or counterproductive to other interests of the organization. In addition, one organization may feel a degree of "ownership" over an activity or technique that another organization plans to use.

- *Identity:* Resistance also occurs when an organization feels that proposed cooperation would adversely affect how it is viewed by other entities both inside and outside the company.

- *Personalities:* Key players, who are personally disliked by other stakeholders because they are perceived to represent a political or organizational threat, can undermine efforts toward collaboration.

Senior Commitment to SAM

After silo mentality, practitioners rated the remaining obstacles to alignment almost equally. But one could argue that there is a strong correlation between the degree of "senior management support" and other factors, such as flaws in compensation design, incorrect allocation of resources, lack of buy-in for the SAM program and even silo mentality. This would explain the overwhelming number of practitioners who have stressed the importance of a SAM program being mandated "from the top" to truly achieve results. It's easy to understand why. It's challenging to get approval for ideas that require reallocating business units' revenue or spending capital dollars without executive support. A CEO who plays an active, visible role regarding SAM initiatives sends a strong message throughout the company regarding their importance, which helps establish the credibility and authority of the program. When senior management makes decisions or exhibits behavior counter to the strategy, however, the results can be disastrous.

"I set up a meeting for the CEO of one of my customers to fly to my firm's headquarters to meet with my boss and our CEO. My boss wouldn't let me come to the meeting because of the expense! The customer wanted me there and offered to pay for my travel; my boss and the CEO still wouldn't let me come. After the meeting, which our CEO bungled, the customer CEO came to me and said, 'Based on what your CEO said, it is clear to us that your company really doesn't care about us.'"

The ability to leverage senior management at the executive / client interface gives a strong differential advantage over the competition. Conversely, in an age when buying decisions are getting made at higher levels, lack of senior executive support and participation can be the cause of lost business.

What Does Misalignment Cost You?

As we've noted, it takes the efforts of an entire organization to enable a supplier to deliver customer value. In order to manage the "wallet of the future" effectively, the SAM must embed his company in the customer's decision-making process as it relates to jointly creating new opportunities for both firms. When there is misalignment inside a supplier organization, it is incredibly tough to respond to either of the two critical mandates of leading customers today.

Customer Mandate #1: "Make It Easier for Us to Do Business with You!"

If you had a nickel for every time someone in your customer's organization said this to you, you would be enjoying early retirement. The stories of dysfunction are rampant and surprisingly similar across diverse companies. The reality is, even routine delivery of goods and services has become difficult in a today's complex environment.

The Loyalty Effect by Frederick F. Reichheld describes how companies lose 10% of their account base every year because of "inadequate account management." In fact, effective account management is fast emerging as one of the primary barriers-of-entry to competitors. Not only is it a fundamental way to combat price competition without lowering prices as well, but superior account management can often command higher prices, or at the very least, produce systems efficiencies that result in reduced costs of doing business and better margins. But without the proper infrastructure to support collaboration, merely allocating additional people to more effectively manage an account often fails to provide better customer service, and can even decrease efficiency while raising the cost of sales. This is simply because the more people involved in an account, the greater the complexity, and without any way to harness that complexity, it is tough to provide the levels of service promised.

In today's selling environment, account managers are being asked to manage all customer interactions and ensure the entire team is providing high quality responses and content on time—while *at the same time* being asked to play a strategic role in devising ways to sell deeper and wider into the account. Unfortunately, today's intricate corporate web of structures and relationships has created *huge* issues of coordination, consistency and responsiveness. AMR Research found that approximately 40% of an entire account team's time is spent on day-to-day team coordination activities, and *not* on strategic selling. With the strategic or global account manager, it's even worse. They struggle with how to drive increased results in a shorter timeframe and at a lower cost. This is virtually impossible when, according to a recent SAMA study, the average account manager is only able to spend 11% of his or her time on sales activities, and total time working with customers is limited to 25% due to all of the coordination responsibilities inherent in the role. One *Fortune 1000* high-tech company told us about how it had been prevented from penetrating deeper into an established account where it was already engaged with ten divisions. While it had done an excellent job of selling into the account, one of its deployments with a division had not been served in a timely manner by its operations team, leading to frustration and a loss of credibility with the customer. This company's competitor was able to use that situation as a reason to displace it on a new multi-million dollar contract within that customer account!

Customer Mandate #2: "IMPACT My Strategy, My Bottom Line and My Own Customers"

I think Neil Rackham summarized it best when he said that yesterday's sales force *communicated* value to its customers while today's sales force *creates* value for its customers. The fact remains that most value added in businesses today is in the form of knowledge, not materials. Experts estimate that knowledge accounts for 75% of the value added even in manufacturing. Unfortunately, what all too many companies ignore is that organizations leverage knowledge through networks of people who collaborate—not through networks of technology that interconnect. The challenge is, therefore, a cultural one, not a technical one, because true value creation is dependent upon not only access to the right information at the right time, but to a culture of collaboration inside the firm.

> **Alignment + Collaboration = Value Creation**

The IT graveyard is littered with companies that followed high budget, "visionary" CIOs down the path of this or that client-server investment, or rolled out new e-mail systems, only to find that people still didn't want to collaborate to share and develop new knowledge. Bottom line—interconnectivity begins with people who want to connect. After that, tools and technology can make the connection. Employees are competitive by nature, and may be more inclined to hoard, rather than share, knowledge they have. Some have even referred to knowledge transfer as a body-contact sport.

One office-equipment manufacturer sought to increase the rate of "knowledge-transfer" among its departments while simultaneously downsizing the workforce. The combination proved impossible. Who wants to share what they know when the boss is looking to cut headcount and consolidate expertise in a smaller and cheaper organization? The truth is, we have a tendency to guard what we know. We think that what we know is what really continues to provide us with long-term employment. So how do we get people to share information?

Executing a knowledge-based strategy is not about managing knowledge; it's about nurturing people with knowledge. People will not willingly share information with coworkers if their workplace culture does not support learning, cooperation and openness. Because knowledge sharing is not something that occurs naturally, it must be managed, encouraged and rewarded. Employees have to be induced to make "deposits" into whatever knowledge repository your company supports, either through reward or even punishment. One often-cited case study, Buckman Labs, ultimately landed on a carrot-and-stick balance, mixing visible incentives with invisible pressure, and an organization-wide bias toward teamwork and knowledge reciprocity. As one carrot, CEO Bob Buckman organized a one-time event in Scottsdale, Arizona at a fashionable resort as a celebration to recognize the 150 best knowledge-sharers. Those selected received a new IBM ThinkPad 755, a leather computer bag and listened to a presentation by Tom Peters. Within the company, the high-profile event – dubbed "The 4th Wave" – sparked a good deal of discussion, particularly among those who failed to make the cut. The event served its purpose: in the weeks afterward, participation on the company's information-sharing forums increased dramatically.

A strong culture of internal collaboration has a frequently overlooked side-effect that is particularly attractive to those managing strategic customers—it decreases competition amongst stakeholders inside an organization and gets everyone pulling in the same direction (that of the customer). In the most successful firms, a culture of collaboration is simply fundamental to the way the company does business, intrinsic to its operation and embedded as an expression of the company's value system. Looking back, Buckman says that incorporating the knowledge transfer system into a corporate culture is at least a three-year process. "The first year they think you're crazy. The second year they start to see, and in the third year you get buy-in," says Buckman. "What you need is persistence. This whole thing is a journey."

Summary

In this chapter, we worked our way backwards from the forces at work shaping customer strategies, examining how those same forces contribute to the difficulties that suppliers are having in successfully responding. Unfortunately, there is no silver bullet...no straightforward template...no perfect strategy or process that will magically dissolve these complex challenges. But as you read on, you will see that there are highly practical means to improve your performance NOW.

Chapter 2:
Delivering on the Promise:
A Recipe for Change

"I think the best account managers are the ones who can sniff out the opportunities with customer business problems that we can add value to, match the resources of the corporation around the world, get people to all pull in the same direction and translate it into action."

Vice President Global Accounts, Fortune 50 Corporation

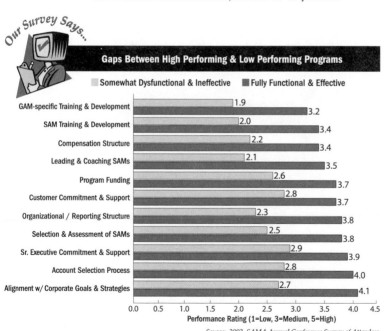

Source: 2002, SAMA Annual Conference Survey of Attendees.

As the chart above shows, even the best organizations perform well below their potential across all SAM program elements. There's good news embedded in those statistics—not only are you not alone in the challenges you grapple with, but your ability to make incremental improvements in these areas can give your company a significant advantage over your competitors. Organizational issues like those explored in **Chapter 1** are common roadblocks to successful execution of SAM strategy. When left unaddressed, they not only contribute to missed opportunities, but pose serious threats to the security of your key customer relationships. In some cases, management has concluded that the failure to see a return on the significant investment made in strategic account management is because the strategy itself is flawed. But if you're reading this, you know that is not where the problem resides. It is the *implementation* of SAM strategies that most firms struggle with, and given the massive shift required to focus your entire organization outwardly on the customer, this isn't a surprise. There are a variety of actions an organization can take to foster an environment in which SAM strategy can best function. This chapter outlines those actions, providing ideas on how account managers can further these messages that will spark change, foster enthusiasm and create momentum. Finding ways to have this kind of IMPACT inside your own company is what will allow you to have more IMPACT with your customers.

What Does It Look Like When You Have IMPACT?

Our Survey Says...

What Does It Look Like When You Have IMPACT Inside Your Own Company?

- *I have identified key decision-makers and have excellent communication between them and the customer.*
- *Everyone wants to work on my team; we have team spirit.*
- *We have alignment with objectives and clear agreement and action on outcomes.*
- *I've created some kind of change and someone else understands my point of view.*
- *We achieve a paradigm shift from being a product company to a customer value company.*
- *I mobilize cross-functional work teams to lend resources toward strategic relationships with high value accounts.*
- *I achieve growth in account share and increase in profitability with key customers.*
- *Other functional organizations in my company support projects and activities for my team's customers.*
- *Alignment is achieved, effectiveness is gained, customers are satisfied and business objectives are met.*

In preparation for this book, SAMA surveyed a cross-section of strategic sales executives to collect some ideas about what it means to have IMPACT. If you read their comments on the previous page closely, you'll see that not one description of IMPACT can be achieved in a vacuum—each one requires a good degree of contribution from other parts of the company. No doubt, you have your own wish list of how you would like to generate IMPACT. Chances are, you already have a good idea of where the weaknesses are in your firm that are putting up roadblocks to prevent it. Now that you've had a chance to contemplate the 50,000 ft. view of the challenges of the current business climate, bring your thinking closer to home and consider the following actions you can take, or encourage others to take:

Actions completely within your sphere of influence and control

- Understand your company's structure (core functions, systems and processes, as well as how they relate to each other and where they overlap).

- Identify current and future issues and challenges of each function and how you can support them effectively.

- Develop relationships with people in each function and cultivate a broad internal network to exchange ideas and rally support.

- Learn from people who have led cross-functional initiatives.

Actions that are more challenging and require additional support

- Establish top down commitment and support for strategic accounts.

- Provide a quantifiable value to the SAM program.

- Design review and compensation programs that put the customer before the need to make quota, plan or P&L targets.

"The account manager used to be like the gatekeeper. The success or failure of the account strategy relied on their credibility. Now they are more of an orchestrator; it's their job to get resource managers inside of the opportunity so they can internalize it themselves."

Best Practice

"I was assigned to a bank that was involved in a political scandal and was on the verge of bankruptcy. As a result, they could not upgrade their technology. The local operational units of my company had begun to de-invest in the account. I asked the bank, 'What if we took over your IT?' I convinced the bank and the government, and the result was a five-year, $230 million dollar outsourcing deal. I did not have the authority to do this. I went in without the support of leadership and made the deal happen when most people would have walked away. I used leadership skills (not authority) to get people who don't talk to each other to build a team and create a value proposition for the customer."

The Controversial Idea: SAMs Need to Become *More* Internally Focused

In order to get your company more focused on the customer, you have to be more focused on your company and all its working (or broken) parts. Your customer expects you to be an advocate whose sphere of influence extends to key individuals in those areas of your company that IMPACT them. Salespeople want to spend time with the customer—NOT inside their own organization fighting battles. We couldn't agree more. But when parts of your company aren't as focused on the customer as they should be, the remedy is to spend time with them, lobbying on your customer's behalf. The work you'll need to do might take just as long as the time you feel you're wasting right now—maybe even longer during the initial steps. The difference is that it will be quality time that will lay a foundation for more efficient and effective internal collaboration over time.

Focusing internally does not have to be at the expense of the customer—it should be on behalf of the customer.

Our Survey Says...

What Do You Need to Learn to Have Greater IMPACT Within Your Own Company?

- *How to get my entire organization to behave as a true alliance / value team with our customers.*
- *How to build relationships prior to needing them for a project.*
- *How to achieve senior management commitment.*
- *How to work within the silo structure and combat territorialism.*
- *How to motivate back office support to become more customer-focused.*
- *How to challenge internal inertia.*
- *How to get my company to act as a "whole" instead of individual units, and to coordinate company objectives across multiple levels.*
- *How to get the entire organization to "rally" around the customer.*
- *How to create a win / win for supplier and customer.*
- *How to effectively do the "internal" sale.*
- *How to instill the same sense of urgency to meet the customer's need in others that the SAM brings from the customer meeting.*
- *How to overcome resistance in my own organization.*

Navigating and Managing the Silos

Chapter 1 focused heavily on alignment challenges related to turf issues. It articulated the problem and its source—now it's time to start thinking about a plan of action. Silos can, in fact, be navigated and managed, but it's critical to understand them first. In order to effectively build relationships within them, you need to understand their organizational priorities. Remember that silos will never evaporate—complex firms *need* silos in order to operate. Your strategy is not to beat down the silo walls, but rather to work to a win-win solution. As you build your knowledge of them, and theirs of you, you can even create customer advocates of them.

Chapter 1 outlined a variety of sources of turf battles. Refer to that list, as well as the skill-building tools in **PART II**, when you are attempting to diagnose a current problem or perform a post-mortem on a past struggle. Of course, negotiating your way out of a turf battle is not nearly as desirable as having none to deal with at all! It's certainly not the most productive way to focus your attention internally. Identifying ways to avoid turf battles in the first place is more than worth the time it will save you in the end, and a good example of the types of internal activities you want to migrate toward in the future. Some ways to avoid turf battles include:

- *Engage in Consensus Building:* Don't underestimate the time required to clarify coalition goals and develop each person's commitment to them. The higher the sense of common purpose, the higher the probability of harmonious relations between colleagues. This includes agreeing upon definitions of success that are meaningful to *all* constituents.

- *Focus on Being Capacity-Centered Rather Than Problem-Centered:* Clearly connecting the needs relative to the potential available resources can help build early momentum and cooperation.

- *Understand the Stakeholders:* Knowing the relationship between personal goals, silo goals and the overall corporate goals can reveal potential sources of agreement and disagreement. Remember that collaboration must produce benefits for all participants.

- *Adopt a Spirit of Compromise:* A group's goals are never 100% compatible with the goals of each organization or person involved.

Common Ground Coupled with a Sense of Urgency

What is it that brings people together in ways rarely or never before seen? **Common Ground**. Researchers at Booz-Allen believe that the world has entered a new age – an Age of Collaboration – where self-reliance is not an option. In their comprehensive global study of cross-border alliances and alliance practices (covering 5,500

> "I spend a lot of my time converting headquarters relationships into a set of headquarters plus local relationships. I am not at all trying to compete with the local sales teams in terms of quality of relationship...the truth is, there's not enough of me to go around. The local teams are critical to my success because I can't get to all those countries as often as I'd like, so I need them to have the very best relationship that they can."

alliances and more than 500 companies), they demonstrate that alliances – particularly those between supplier and customer – result in higher returns to those companies proficient in alliance building. The key to their proficiency is **Common Ground**.

Sometimes, though, it can be difficult to build coalitions even when all stakeholders can find a **Common Ground**. Management guru John Kotter, who has exhaustively studied both success and failure in change initiatives in business, outlines eight distinct phases of successful change initiatives. **Sense of Urgency** is number one. According to Kotter, talk of change in business typically begins with some people noticing vulnerability in the organization. The threat of losing ground in some way sparks these people into action, and they in turn try to communicate that **Sense of Urgency** to others. Kotter notes that over half the companies he has observed have never been able to create enough urgency to prompt action. "Without motivation, people won't help and the effort goes nowhere," says Kotter, "executives underestimate how hard it can be to drive people out of their comfort zones." How much urgency is enough to prompt a new order of things? Kotter suggests it is when 75% of your leadership is honestly convinced that business as usual is no longer an acceptable plan. As you build internal allies, you will undoubtedly be searching for a source of **Common Ground** amongst stakeholders, which points squarely towards the customer. Just don't forget to instill a **Sense of Urgency** to take action.

Getting Your SAM Program Director More Involved in Facilitating Change

Much of this book is focused on providing a framework to help you work with, and even around, the inherent organizational barriers that exist inside your company, because breaking down or removing those barriers is not typically within the purview of a SAM. At least not directly, that is. You *can* exert influence on your SAM Program Director who *does* have some leverage to rectify the processes (or lack thereof) that are preventing you from being customer-focused. While **Part II** of this book focuses on skills and tools useful for SAMs, the principles of IMPACT without authority apply to your supervisors as well! Many of the tools and methods to assist you in making a business case for action and marshalling support will help your SAM Program Director do the same with the many stakeholders with whom he or she must engage. In addition, **Part III**, of this book is written directly to senior management, and addresses the role it must play in removing the organizational obstacles that impede effective strategic account management. Buy your boss a book, or pass yours on, but make sure they are at the top of your action list. Even if they are already an active, vocal advocate, they, too, will appreciate some fresh ideas on how to be more customer-focused as a company.

Best Practice

"During the beginning of our initial program, it was most critical to gain support from our executive office before we launched a customer initiative. Our process went as follows for building the case for a SAM program with our Executive Office:

Create a Shared Need

- The reason to change, whether driven by threat or opportunity, is instilled within the organization and widely shared through data, demonstration, demand or diagnosis.
- What were the benefits (financial) to the corporation, individual SBUs, sales professionals and customers?
- Benchmark study: Results of other companies with similar size compared with our strategy.
- How we would overcome issues that could prevent our success.
- What are the competitive advantages and differentiations over our competition?

Shaping the Vision

- The desired outcome of change is clear, legitimate, widely understood and shared.
- Involved cross-functional team to support communication, direction and benefits within their business.
- Target and profile customers by segment that best fit our capabilities and abilities to serve.
- Created incentive program (outside of normal compensation) for sales representatives.

Mobilizing Commitment

- There is a strong commitment from key constituents to invest in the change, make it work and demand and receive management attention.
- Identify EO member as our sponsor for program.
- Each member of the Senior Lead Team took responsibility for developing a specific number of customers across the enterprise.
- Identify key stakeholder within each business who took ownership of cross-divisional customer.

Making Change Last

- Once change is started, it endures, flourishes and learnings are transferred throughout the organization.
- Create database to measure results cross-divisionally.
- Communicate on monthly basis to Senior Leaders how their customers are doing.

Monitor Progress

- Progress is real; benchmarks set and realized; indicators established to guarantee accountability.
- Measured success (e.g. revenue, profit, account share)."

A Word About Your CEO

Even the chief sales executive does not possess enough influence to truly drive institutional relationships. The true point of leverage resides within the Executive Suite—a place devoid of silo loyalty, possessing a broader view and a long-term vision. Setting aside the obvious reality that CEOs are pressured by the short-term performance climate we are all dealing with, the CEO is where the buck stops, and most of them are keen to identify the inefficiencies inside their own organization.

Chapter 10 delivers you a tool to "influence up" in your organization on behalf of the SAM program, and more importantly, the customer. In this chapter, the responsibility of the Executive Suite in enabling customer focus is made abundantly clear in a direct manner backed up by compelling quantitative and qualitative evidence. Our aim is to help you convince your CEO that your own organizational processes and structures are inhibiting customer focus, derailing superior delivery of good and services and stalling innovation. Armed with this information, and some serious homework on your firm's particular challenges, you will be better positioned to make a strong business case inside your company for fixing these issues.

We've written this chapter directly to your CEO, even providing a stand-alone version of **Chapter 10** so that you can hand it to your top decision-makers as opposed to handing them this entire book.* We also realize that you may prefer to absorb the argument yourself and find less direct ways of filtering it where it needs to go inside your organization. How you decide to utilize this chapter will depend entirely on the role you play within your company, the degree of management support your firm currently enjoys, and the amount of risk you are willing and able to take in order to make strategic account management an Executive Suite priority.

* *A copy of the stand-alone* **Message to the CEO** *was originally included with this book. If you'd like another one, please contact SAMA at 312-251-3131.*

Summary

As you prepare to discover the steps and acquire the skills to achieve IMPACT without authority, you may be a bit skeptical of your ability as a single individual to effect change within your firm. Management guru Peter Senge has a theory about why companies have historically had such difficulty changing. "The majority of strategic initiatives that are led from the top are marginally effective at best," notes Senge. "How many reorganizations actually produce companies that are dramatically more effective than they were before?" Senge believes the problem lies in the "company-as-machine" model that is our current paradigm for both operating and changing firms. "You have a broken company, and you need to change it, to fix it," explains Senge. "But companies are living organisms, not machines. That might explain why it is so difficult for us to succeed in our efforts to produce change. We keep bringing in mechanics—when what we need are gardeners. We keep trying to drive change—when what we need to do is *cultivate* change."

Senge's hypothesis about the best way to begin fostering change is a powerful one for strategic account managers and their program leaders. Why? Because in Senge's vision, the power of the few is enormous. After studying numerous companies that were able to sustain significant momentum over many years, Senge found that every single change process started very small and centered around "seed carriers," or internal networkers, who knew how to build informal communities within their companies. Over time, ideas spawned by one team spread, percolate and foster new clusters of teams that ultimately create a network that carries change into wider groups.

Here is where Senge's message becomes relevant to you. Over the last 12 years, SAMA has encountered thousands of enthusiastic practitioners who truly understand how their company needs to change in order to become more customer-centric. They attend SAMA conferences, read *Velocity*™ and network with peers in order to find new ways of approaching customer relationships. And often times they get frustrated, because the task of effecting change inside their organization is too daunting, too risky, too tiring, too unrewarding—TOO DIFFICULT. But consider Senge's theory of how true organizational change comes about. As you put your new skills into practice, recruit a pilot group comprised of "believers" who have found a better way of working, and be sure there are real business results being generated. People will be drawn to a network of committed, enthusiastic people who are solving problems and producing results. And just maybe your ideas will take root.

> *"The vision must be followed by the venture. It is not enough to stare up the steps—we must step up the stairs."*
>
> *Vance Havne*

PART II
The Model

Part II
The Model

As we explore how to create impact in situations in which you have no explicit authority, a huge advantage should be emphasized at the start.

As a salesperson, you represent the customer.

How many companies state in their mission "We will *not* be customer-focused"? None, of course. Yet you might often feel like the lone voice in the wilderness advocating for your customer. Remember that your direct link to the customer can and should be used to your advantage. It cannot, however, be your sole strategy. In fact, salespeople who think that representing the customer is sufficient enough to exert internal influence are those who have the most difficulty.

The figure on the next page is PDI's approach to creating impact in the absence of authority. Its depiction as a series of stairs is no accident:

- It's always easier to climb stairs one at a time. You can climb by skipping a stair or two, but that's not always the easiest way to arrive where you want.

- You should start at the bottom of the stairs. Yes, you're probably tempted to skip the first one or two, but it's safer to start at the bottom.

- Sometimes when you're climbing stairs, you need to go back down because you've forgotten something.

- Once you learn to climb, it's fairly automatic. You won't need to think it through each time.

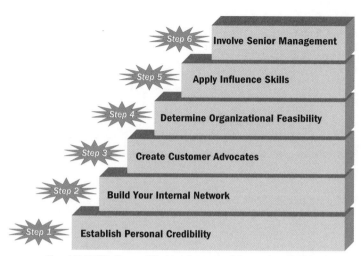

Steps 1 – 3: A Solid Foundation

The first three steps to achieving *IMPACT Without Authority* are part of your ongoing job; they are the preparation you take *in anticipation* of needing to influence others at some point in the future. Even if you have an opportunity *now* that requires you to influence others, you should start with these chapters in order to gain a good understanding of your personal starting point. This exercise will also help you deliberately work to build a more solid foundation for the future.

In any job, you strive to **Establish Personal Credibility**. In **Chapter 3**, your knowledge of the importance of being trusted and viewed as having expertise will be developed. You will explore how others perceive you and how that can contribute to your ability to influence.

You already recognize the significance of building a network when selling to your external customer. It is just as important that you **Build Your Network** in your own organization. **Chapter 4** provides insights into what you need to understand about various stakeholders, as well as how to go about obtaining that knowledge.

You have a huge advantage when trying to influence internally because you represent the external customer. Rather than carrying the torch alone on behalf of your customer, **Chapter 5** will help you

Create Customer Advocates in your company. When others develop a sense of ownership for your customer, you will find your ideas are easier to sell.

Steps 4 – 6: Achieving Buy-In

The skills and processes dealt with in the next three chapters will assist you with specific opportunities that require buy-in from others outside your area of control.

Determining Organizational Feasibility is critical to thoroughly assessing the stakeholders you need to influence. **Chapter 6** focuses on recognizing what others' reactions are apt to be (and why), as well as who you will need to bring in to approve decisions. This will allow you to plan an effective approach with them.

As you **Apply Influence Skills** during your internal selling process, it will be important to adjust your message and your method on a stakeholder-by-stakeholder basis. **Chapter 7** will help you find the real win-win that ensures that you not only get what you are looking for, but simultaneously build trust and a better working relationship so that future conversations become quicker and easier.

Depending on the depth or breadth of change you are trying to achieve, it is quite possible you will need to **Involve Senior Management**. This step is not simply an escalation strategy; it could be an imperative for certain levels of change. **Chapter 8** will help you use senior management more effectively.

Regardless of your current ability to influence without authority, you can never learn too much. Achieving a positive impact for your customers *and* your firm will be the result of the cumulative effect of numerous actions that you've taken. Whether you need to learn more about two of them or thirty-two of them is simply a matter of where your skill levels are today.

Chapter 3:
Establish Personal Credibility

At first glance, you're ready to skip this chapter. After all, you're successful, perhaps you're in one of those positions that dozens of others aspire to reach or you just received a glowing performance appraisal. You "made your numbers," collected your bonus and are getting positive feedback from your customers.

We encourage you to read on.

> *One of the most important things you can do for your customer is to create a foundation of support internally so that it is there before you need to leverage it. This begins with establishing your own personal credibility.*

Customers want to know that you, their SAM, have credibility in your own organization. It helps them feel safe that you can muster the resources and influence necessary to meet their needs.

Challenge yourself to learn how others see you. You will learn a nugget or two about how you are perceived, which will help you to build your credibility and influence. Your advocacy role will be much easier if you are not an "unknown entity" trying to sell your position internally to others.

Let's start with a self-test. When you've completed it, note the questions that resulted in a lower score and keep them in mind as you read the chapter.

	Strongly Disagree	Somewhat Agree	Strongly Agree
	1 - - - - - 2 - - - - - 3 - - - - - 4 - - - - - 5		
1. I do what I say I will do, in the agreed-to timeframes.	1 - - - - - 2 - - - - - 3 - - - - - 4 - - - - - 5		
2. Others perceive me as putting the company's interests above my own.	1 - - - - - 2 - - - - - 3 - - - - - 4 - - - - - 5		
3. I understand how I come across to others, and how that helps or hinders my effectiveness.	1 - - - - - 2 - - - - - 3 - - - - - 4 - - - - - 5		
4. I provide recognition to others for their contributions to my account's success.	1 - - - - - 2 - - - - - 3 - - - - - 4 - - - - - 5		
5. I proactively communicate information about my customer to others who support this customer.	1 - - - - - 2 - - - - - 3 - - - - - 4 - - - - - 5		
6. I am viewed as open and honest, without hidden agendas.	1 - - - - - 2 - - - - - 3 - - - - - 4 - - - - - 5		
7. I consistently achieve the business results expected of me.	1 - - - - - 2 - - - - - 3 - - - - - 4 - - - - - 5		
8. I am recognized within my company for my expertise.	1 - - - - - 2 - - - - - 3 - - - - - 4 - - - - - 5		

How Am I Perceived?

We begin this chapter by encouraging you to examine some of the qualities that make you who you are—and that either encourage or discourage others from working with you.

The following list of adjectives will help you understand how others perceive you—an important step as you think about how your ideas might be received by others. Although your view of yourself will not be as accurate as asking others to provide feedback, self-assessments generally raise awareness.

Remember, there are no right or wrong answers, and you don't have to mark every descriptor. This exercise is meant to make you think about some of your qualities and how they affect your ability to influence others.

√ = I am this way almost all the time
X = I am almost never this way
P = I am this way under pressure

_____ accepting	_____ fair	_____ perfectionist
_____ adaptable	_____ flexible	_____ pessimistic
_____ aggressive	_____ friendly	_____ practical
_____ ambitious	_____ giving	_____ quarrelsome
_____ anxious	_____ helpful	_____ questioning
_____ calm	_____ independent	_____ quiet
_____ cheerful	_____ innovative	_____ reasonable
_____ compromising	_____ introverted	_____ reliable
_____ confident	_____ intuitive	_____ reserved
_____ conforming	_____ irritable	_____ resisting
_____ cooperative	_____ judgmental	_____ responsible
_____ courteous	_____ knowledgeable	_____ sarcastic
_____ critical	_____ logical	_____ serious
_____ demanding	_____ negative	_____ sociable
_____ doubting	_____ nervous	_____ spontaneous
_____ effective	_____ open-minded	_____ tactful
_____ efficient	_____ optimistic	_____ team player
_____ empathetic	_____ organized	_____ tense
_____ energetic	_____ patient	_____ thoughtful
_____ even-tempered	_____ perceptive	_____ uncertain

You might want to complete the following questions from two different perspectives: how those in your immediate work group (e.g., other SAMs) perceive you, versus how people in your company with whom you interact less frequently perceive you.

1. Some of the adjectives that best describe me are:	Some of the adjectives that describe me least well are:	Some of the adjectives that describe me when I am under pressure are:
•	•	•
•	•	•
•	•	•

2. How do my qualities help me when I am trying to influence others?

3. How do my qualities hurt my ability to influence?

4. Which of the adjectives that I display under pressure are not descriptive of me at other times? (Note: These are characteristics that, with some coaching, you could learn to better manage.)

5. When I compare myself to others who I think are able to effectively influence:

 • In what area(s) are we alike?

 • In what area(s) should I focus my development efforts?

 • What is something I should work on, and what will I do about it?

The Importance of Credibility

What does establishing personal credibility mean?

You have credibility when people trust you and acknowledge that you possess the expertise to get things done.

The PDI Credibility Matrix

Your career journey likely started with a role as an "individual contributor." You were responsible for yourself, and you primarily managed tasks. Your expertise, and your ability to develop more of it over time, was a large component of how you were appraised. Your first increase in responsibility was perhaps as a team or project liaison, and then you may have been designated as a team or project leader. As your career progressed further, you gained responsibility for others' results in positions such as sales management.

With each expansion in responsibility, your previous role helped prepare you for the next one. As your expertise grew, what you also realized was that trust and your ability to work through others became increasingly important.

An interesting trend related to the SAM function is the growing desire of organizations to build bench strength internally for this position, versus simply hiring top talent from the outside. Prior to the mid-1990s, the concept of strategic account management was still somewhat overwhelming to many corporations, so the quickest route to implementation was to hire a few experienced SAMs. In many cases these new hires did exactly what was intended—they jumpstarted the corporate SAM program. But in many other cases, the new hires were not successful. The primary reason for this, assuming they really did possess the skills cited on their resume, was that they could not quickly build the internal credibility they needed. They counted on communicating past successes as *the* means to build credibility.

Unfortunately, many other criteria for credibility exist that take time to become established, and new hires must recognize and appreciate the importance of these criteria, no matter their level of competence.

Some companies have an inherent bias against outsiders (what is the average length of service in *your* company?), and as a result it may be an uphill struggle for any new hire. But even in companies that are more accepting of new talent, the timing doesn't always work, or the complexity of the company requires too steep a learning curve. If you're a newly hired SAM, and you've uncovered a great opportunity in your first few months on the job, you may be disappointed to learn that you've had insufficient time to develop the credibility you need to successfully sell your ideas. Having influence is about "who knows you" in addition to what you do and who you know.

Trust

Trust can be complex, but it's not an intangible over which you have no control. It's one of those things that takes a long time to build, and a much shorter time to destroy. To rebuild trust is usually much more difficult than it was to initially construct it, which is why it is so important to maintain trust once you have it. Components of trust addressed in this book are reliability, communication and recognition of others.

Reliability

When thinking about how to build trust, an important component is your follow-through. Do you do what you say you will do? A business executive we know once commented, "There are two types of people in any company. Those who do what they say will do, and those who don't. It's that simple." Which are you? Amazingly, there are so many people who fall into that second category, that it becomes almost too easy to establish credibility simply by being in the first category!

Unless you've asked others for feedback in this area, you may not have an accurate view of how others perceive you. As you find yourself committing to deliverables, think about the following:

Situation	Implication
Do you commit by saying "I'll try to get that done"?	The word "try" is weak and can be perceived as giving yourself an excuse in advance. If you can't be confident about the outcome, a better technique is to state what you will do, while being realistic about potential barriers: "I will contact our customer, but given their resource constraints I'm not confident they will agree to participate."
Do people frequently follow up with you on things you have agreed to do?	This could be a signal they do not trust you to fulfill your commitments.
Do you find yourself saying "yes" to others when you know you should be saying "no"?	You are likely over-committing. When you then cannot deliver, others will lose their trust in you.
If you run into an obstacle that will prevent you meeting a commitment, do you let others know in advance?	It is always more effective to be straightforward about problems than to wait for the due date to offer an explanation. Contact others in advance; don't simply hope the problem will go away.
Do you communicate the outcome of activities you've completed?	Even though it might be obvious to you that you've completed something, it might not be as apparent to others. A quick status update will ensure that others are not left wondering whether you followed through or not.

Building trust through reliability happens over time. What if you're in a situation where time is not available, and your track record is not yet established? The fastest way to build a trusting relationship is by meeting with others face-to-face. Taking the time to travel and meet in person goes a long way toward establishing your own credibility, especially when you are working with colleagues in other geographies.

One of the reasons trust is harder to build cross-culturally is that different norms create a feeling of distrust, sometimes for no other reason than the factor of the "unknown." When you experience being in a culture, you will more easily develop an understanding of the country and its workers—and even the pace at which you can expect to implement new ideas. All that is not possible through e-mail and voice communications. What often happens, too, is that by meeting with your colleagues in other cultures, you discover the goals you have in common. You can use these common goals as a foundation for accomplishing new ideas in the future.

Carrie Rosencrans, Tammy Routh and Marian Goetzman, Alliance Accounts Directors at Marriott International, relate thier experience with building trust across cultures.

"We decided to hold a series of regional meetings that would connect us with our colleagues throughout Asia. The strategic accounts we manage have strong growth in that region of the world, but we had not met face-to-face with many of our Marriott colleagues. Our business is complex, because we have local account managers, plus local hotel personnel with whom we need to develop relationships.

This event took many months to plan, and we started getting acquainted with our colleagues through the planning we did over the telephone and e-mail. One of our colleagues in Asia spent a lot of time preparing us for cultural differences, such as presenting where English is a second language.

The event itself brought everyone to a different level. By actually spending time in that culture, those of us from the U.S. immediately understood what our colleagues had been saying. We better understood the differences in how we conduct business, yet confirmed we share many of the same goals: We all want to grow share and generate more business, and we want to differentiate Marriott from its competitors.

By spending time face-to-face, we developed real relationships with each other. This trip demonstrated our commitment to our internal colleagues. In our industry, things happen differently when there is a relationship, and this event did more to build internal partnerships than any e-mail messages, newsletters or even corporate mandates could have."

In addition to getting others to trust you, another important outcome is achieved.

You will enhance your trust of others in your own company.

You've all had the experience of sitting in your customer's office, wondering whether you can really count on some other part of your company to come through. As you make an effort to increase others' trust in you, think too of what you need to do to increase your trust in them. You want to be able to speak confidently of your entire global organization, and by engaging with the organization you will.

Trusting relationships are also established and sustained by each party's willingness to appreciate the other's needs. Others will grant you greater trust if you are clear about your intentions and agenda, and if they believe what you say. You build trust when others believe that you understand *their* interests. Honesty and the appreciation of mutual interests are the baseline of any long-term relationship. Chapters 4 and 7 provide tools to help you build that appreciation across other entities and individuals.

Another important aspect of trust is to demonstrate to others that you place the company's interests above your own—which also translates into putting the company's interests above those of your customer. It is, unfortunately, all too easy for salespeople to gain a reputation for "selling out" to their customer. Even if you have thought through your ideas and have a solid business case that demonstrates benefits for both your customer and your company, not everyone is aware of those details. They only hear that you're asking for something that will benefit your customer. Your goal is to demonstrate balance: You are a customer advocate as well as a company advocate. Chapters 6 and 8 will guide you in that balance.

Communications

Critical to building trust is communicating with others. This is especially important with those parts of your company that have direct relationships with your customer and are concerned about how their role might change.

Successful SAMs will tell you a very simple rule about communications.

There is no such thing as over-communicating!

Communicating only what others "need to know" is not communicating enough. As a SAM, you possess an abundance of information about the customer, and you might be considering a variety of ideas for growing the account. You may feel that it is not relevant to share information or ideas with other parts of the organization until they need to get directly involved. There are two problems with this approach:

- By not openly sharing information, you will be perceived as withholding information. You might not *think* you are withholding, but others will view the situation differently.

- You will be missing out on the power of others' thinking. The more information you share, the more the potential for the emergence of ideas from others. And if others are involved with developing an idea for something new or different, it will be that much easier to gain buy-in to implementing that idea.

"When I first got involved in national account management seven or eight years ago, the first year we were in existence as an organization we made 350 presentations. Of those 350 presentations, 300 were internal."

Whereas the old-school definition of "knowledge is power" implied that closely-held knowledge placed you above others, a more contemporary adage should be "shared knowledge is power." The respect and buy-in you gain from others will benefit you far more than the withholding of information.

When you meet with your account team (or anyone who interfaces with your account), be sure they understand why your account was chosen to be a strategic account. This provides both a better understanding of the account as well as of your company's expectations of that account. Ask them what kinds of information they would like to know now, what kinds of information they want on an ongoing basis and the best method of communicating it. Even if they can't think of things at that time, they will appreciate being asked. Later, route information that they have either requested or that you think would be interesting to them.

It's also important that account team members keep you and each other informed. In fact, a good exercise to do with your team is to brainstorm the following questions:

- *What kinds of information do we need to communicate with each other?*

- *What kinds of information need to be communicated with the SAM?*

For example, keep others informed about meetings you have with the customer. By sharing what you have learned, you will build the knowledge base of others, which in turn will enable them to contribute more ideas. On the other hand, team members do not necessarily need to let everyone know about *every* meeting they have. Criteria for identifying which meetings need to be shared might include those that move the team toward its goals, that uncover opportunities or that deal with issues about which you need to be aware.

There will be times when you cannot share certain knowledge. You might become privy to sensitive information about your customer's acquisition strategies, economic troubles or new product launches. When you can't share something, simply say so. People will understand.

Recognition of Others

Giving positive recognition to others is another strategy for building credibility in your own organization.

By recognizing others' contributions to your account, you raise those individuals' trust in you.

Remember, you are in a position with broad levels of responsibility, and there could very well be people in your company who feel

---

that, simply by virtue of your position, you have taken something away from them. This happens particularly often in the field sales organization. By recognizing colleagues' contributions to your account, you will build their trust that you put others' interests above your own. In addition, they will appreciate you giving credit where credit is due. One more result: by recognizing others, you also increase your own visibility within the organization. This visibility creates broader awareness of your customer and the SAM program as well.

As explained on page 32 when the IMPACT Without Authority model was first introduced, the first three steps are about creating a foundation of support that will be there when you seek buy-in to your new ideas. Recognition is a motivator, and often the people you recognize are the very people from whom you will be asking for more support at a later point in time.

Whom to Recognize

There are a myriad of opportunities for recognition of the employees who have contributed to account success, and that positive recognition will help to motivate those parts of the organization from whom you need support.

Employee recognition should start with the sales cycle. For example, think about your initial "win" of the account. The following questions will help you identify whom to recognize as contributing to this success:

- *Who identified this lead? Who helped you in your discovery process?*

- *Did any other function or person help to craft the proposal? Or develop the solution?*

- *With whom did your customer meet, other than you, during the sales process?*

- *What features of your company contributed to winning the account?*

Recognition should continue as the account relationship continues. If there is an implementation or start-up phase, the milestone of completing that phase is another good time to convey your appreciation.

The day-to-day delivery and service providers to your account should also be recognized periodically. These are the employees who ensure your company "meets requirements" so that you have the time, and your customer gives you the opportunity, to climb higher up the relationship hierarchy (see also page 55).

As you identify opportunities to expand what you provide your customer, think of the people in your company who helped make the initiative successful. Ask yourself the following questions:

- *Who helped you shape a new solution? E.g., Product management? Engineering? R&D?*

- *Who needed to develop new processes to support a custom need? Manufacturing? Distribution?*

- *Did sales or marketing implement a different practice to support the new deliverable?*

- *Did IT develop a custom application for something you needed?*

- *Did anyone "jump through hoops" to meet a unique customer need?*

Forms of Recognition

As you provide recognition to employees who have contributed to account success, think in terms of:

- Personal acknowledgements; and

- Public acknowledgements.

Personal acknowledgements. It is so easy to thank individuals for their contributions to your account, and yet it is also so easy to forget to do it. The quickest method is generally an e-mail message or voice mail message. For stronger effect, send a short hand-written note. Stopping by someone's office, or leaving a post-it note on their telephone or computer, will demonstrate that their efforts are appreciated.

When you visit your customer, let them know of the different people in your organization who have come together on their behalf. Ask for some of their company logo items such as pens, t-shirts and other trinkets. Giving these things to the people in your organization will let them know you acknowledged their contributions to your customer.

Public acknowledgements. Letting people know one-on-one they are appreciated is important in building relationships, but letting others know of their contributions is generally even more powerful. The first step to doing this is to let the person's boss know the significance of the contribution that was made. You can simply "cc" the person's boss on that e-mail message you sent to the employee, or leave a duplicate of the voice mail message you sent.

For exceptional contributions, ask your customer to write a letter recognizing the efforts that were made on their behalf. You might even provide the names of individuals or functions that should be mentioned, so that when you receive the letter you can pass along copies to the appropriate employees as well as their bosses.

When thinking about public recognition, remember that there are some folks who do not want to be publicly recognized. In addition, recognition practices vary across cultures. Learn in advance what the appropriate approach should be, so that you do not embarrass others or yourself.

If appropriate for the situation, determine how the employee's work group provides recognition:

- *Is it through group meetings? If so, and you can be there, attend the appropriate part of the meeting where you can say a few words about what the employee did.*

- *Is there a location, such as a bulletin board, where employee performance is recognized? Find out how you can contribute something to the board.*

- *Is there a group newsletter of some form? Again, find out how you can use it to recognize individuals, or perhaps even the entire function or site. Provide quotes from the customer, or include a copy of the recognition letter they sent.*

- *Are top performers recognized at some kind of event? Find out who will be recognized at these events, and if someone you too want to recognize is in the group, see if you can contribute to the words that will be spoken about them.*

An important note about public recognition at events: It requires good preparation! We've all seen it happen where some executive stands in front of a large group of employees and delivers praise in an insincere way. Help the presenter be specific and accurate, including:

- Correct pronunciation of the employee's name.
- What they did—i.e. what role did they play?
- The impact they had—i.e., why did they make a difference?

Chapter 9, which contains ideas for the Vice President of Strategic Accounts, also addresses how to implement a company-wide recognition program.

To further develop your own insights about trust, complete the following questions.

Who are your "role models" of trusting business relationships?

What did they do to earn your trust?

Have you ever had to earn the trust of people who initially mistrusted you?

What did you do?

Action Plan: Think of yourself.

- What do you need to do to build trust from others who do not know you well?

- What do you need to do to increase trust levels from those who do know you?

- Do you need to re-earn trust from anyone? What steps will you take?

Expertise

Trust is "a necessary but not sufficient" component of building credibility. You also need to assure others that you know what you are doing. When you seek support from others, they will be more likely to rally behind your ideas if they believe you have the knowledge, judgment and ability to make the right decisions and get the job done. They also want to know that your customer respects your expertise and the solutions you offer. They want to be assured that working on your ideas will be worth it. Building that view of yourself is, again, some of the groundwork you should be laying along the way.

One indicator that others use to assess your expertise is simply: Can people count on you to exceed, or at least meet, your goals? It's a lot easier for someone who is exceeding expectations to get positive visibility in any organization. Think about the top performers throughout your company. You might know the names of the top performers in other divisions, even if you don't fully understand what the division does and wouldn't recognize those stars if they walked into your office today. When they also establish trust levels, top performers have a head start when it comes to creating IMPACT without authority; their ideas will be viewed more positively at the outset and they will command others' attention more easily.

On the other hand, if you're consistently in the bottom 25% of performers, you will have to work all the harder to establish credibility. It may not be that you're viewed negatively because you're not a top performer (although that, in fact, may be the case), but rather you haven't appeared on the radar screens of people with whom you don't directly interface. When people don't know you, they don't recognize you as a credible source of ideas. Thus, you have to work harder to have your ideas viewed positively.

Meeting or not meeting goals is a proxy for what's really important. And what's really important is whether you have the skills and abilities to accomplish your job responsibilities.

The role of strategic account manager has often been compared to that of a general manager. Regardless of the complexity of your company or your customer, you need to possess a broad set of skills to be effective.

Some of the specific competencies that others consider when assessing your expertise are the areas of customer knowledge and business / market knowledge, including financial acumen.

"What makes a good SAM? I think the best ones are the ones who can sniff out the opportunities with customer business problems that we can add value to, and then match the resources of the corporation around the world and get people to all pull in the same direction and translate it into action."
Vice President Global Accounts, Fortune 50 Corporation

Customer Knowledge	Business Knowledge
· How well do I understand my customer's business? Its industry? Its supply chain?	· Do I stay current on advancements in my professional field and my industry?
· Do I understand the structure and workings of my customer's organization?	· Do I understand the trends and events that may impact my own company's business?
· Do I understand my customer's challenges?	· Do I understand the impact of global trends on my industry?
· Have I formed relationships at varying functions and levels, including the executive level, within the customer's organization?	· How well do I know my own competitors and their place in the market?
· Do I know how to identify growth opportunities within accounts?	· Am I able to analyze market information to evaluate account opportunities?
· Do I know how to develop unique and creative solutions?	· Do I understand the key factors that affect a company's financial position?
· Are my solutions based on long-term value to the customer and to my company's strategic objectives?	· Can I apply financial analysis to evaluate strategic choices and options?
· Do I know how decisions are made?	· Do I understand the financial impact of decisions on both my customer's and my own company?

As you seek answers to the questions above, ask yourself how visible your expertise is in your company. Even if you feel confident of your expertise, your lack of establishing it with others will result in your being less credible than you perhaps deserve.

Summary

This chapter contained many approaches for introspection. Three parting questions for you:

1. Think about other people in your company who you willingly support. What is it that they have done that makes you feel like you would "do anything for them"?

2. On the other hand, what have others done that resulted in you feeling that you would never want to work with them?

3. What can you do to be more like the people, who you'd unconditionally support, in the first question?

Chapter 4:
Build Your Internal Network

As many a SAM has related,

"I spend more time selling to my own organization than I do to my customer."

What's interesting about this statement is that the techniques that salespeople have learned for selling strategically to their *external* customers are often overlooked when they attempt to sell *internally*. Many of the same principles regarding understanding buyers and their priorities apply, and this chapter will help you adapt them to your organization.

One global account manager (GAM) described the importance of building your internal network in this way:

"What's really important to the customer is how well you understand your own company. It's not so much that the customer is expecting you to know that this widget has 2.35 units of tolerance. The customer is expecting you to know who in your company has the ability to solve problems and create customer solutions. So the expectation is more than "know your product", which is a given, but know your company well enough that you can get any answers and solutions."

As you complete the following self-test, keep the low-scoring questions in mind as you read on.

	Strongly Disagree 1 - - - 2 - - - 3 - - - 4 - - - 5	Somewhat Agree	Strongly Agree
1. I have allies in the key divisions that support my customers (e.g., field sales, distribution, manufacturing, customer / technical support, engineering, product management, IT, etc.)	1 - - - - - - 2 - - - - - - 3 - - - - - - 4 - - - - - - 5		
2. I understand how those key divisions are measured.	1 - - - - - - 2 - - - - - - 3 - - - - - - 4 - - - - - - 5		
3. I understand how their results will be impacted by changes I have proposed, or want to propose.	1 - - - - - - 2 - - - - - - 3 - - - - - - 4 - - - - - - 5		
4. I know who can make various levels of decisions within each of the key divisions.	1 - - - - - - 2 - - - - - - 3 - - - - - - 4 - - - - - - 5		
5. I give something of benefit (e.g., knowledge, information, contacts) to other divisions.	1 - - - - - - 2 - - - - - - 3 - - - - - - 4 - - - - - - 5		
6. I am able to accomplish basic levels of change / customization for my customer fairly easily.	1 - - - - - - 2 - - - - - - 3 - - - - - - 4 - - - - - - 5		

Who Should Be in Your Internal Network?

As you work through the ideas in this chapter, you will identify many touch-points between your company and your customer. In addition, there are other internal entities that you need to understand and build relationships with. Your network should include:

• Functional organizations—e.g., manufacturing, customer service;

• Geographic units—e.g., countries, regions; and

• Business units that sell, or could sell, to your customer.

Consider PDI's Customer Relationship Hierarchy, which illustrates the steps to achieving customer loyalty.

PDI's Customer Relationship Hierarchy

LOYALTY

OFFENSE

Gain Customer Commitment

Meet Customer Needs

Anticipate Customer Needs

Exceed Customer Expectations

SATISFACTION

DEFENSE

Meet Customer Requirements

Determine Customer Requirements and Expectations

Identify Customer by Organization · by Key Contacts

Copyright © 1992, Personnel Decisions International Corporation. All Rights Reserved.

Further condensing the levels of the hierarchy makes it more clear who does what within your organization and how various levels of accountability are covered.

Who's Responsible

Copyright © 2000, Personnel Decisions International Corporation. All Rights Reserved.

"All I have is passion for the client, and a network to help me get things done."

As a SAM, you are responsible for creating the strategic vision of what your relationship with the customer could be. To be visionary, you must be able to anticipate and meet your customers' *needs*, which are different from their *requirements*. Other parts of your company are structured around meeting customers' requirements and exceeding their expectations.

To illustrate these differences, suppose you sell product, as well as service agreements for that product. Your company has several divisions, and the customers of various divisions do overlap. You are responsible for one of those overlapping customers.

- The customer's *requirements* are those things that can be reflected in their RFP (request for proposal) and your company's contracting process. Included are such items as product specifications, delivery times, servicing times, volume pricing, returns procedures and options to upgrade. Both your customer and your company track compliance to these agreements, and quarterly report cards might be used to reflect performance.

  Requirements are at the bottom of the hierarchy because they provide the foundation on which you can grow the account, not because they are less important. In fact, meeting requirements is "the ante to play the game," or rather to doing business, with your customer. If you can't meet these minimum requirements to the satisfaction of your customer, it will find another supplier who can. In addition, if you're not meeting these basic requirements, your customer will question why it should trust your company to fulfill a broader set of deliverables, which your vision might entail.

- Whenever your customer interacts with your company, there is an opportunity to make an impression—and hopefully you are making positive impressions. In fact, your ability to exceed customers' expectations lies in your ability to interact with them in a way that goes beyond the requirements. While we refer to the "meeting requirements" level as *what* you deliver, the "exceeding expectations" level is *how* you deliver it. For example, is the service technician professional, friendly and helpful? Is the customer service representative knowledgeable and able to solve the problem the first time? Is an order mix-up easily resolved? Is the account manager easily reached, and does he consistently follow-through? These are examples of *exceeding expectations* and how your customer-interface people allow you to do more than simply "fulfill requirements."

- Suppose you recognize an opportunity to reduce shipping costs by making some changes in how your company's divisions warehouse and distribute product. This would mean shorter delivery times for your customer and decreased shipping costs. It could also mean increased sales, because these discussions will open the door to discussions about how another division's products might be used. You recognize your customer's *need* for greater flexibility in its product, and you believe your solution both meets that need and will benefit your company.

The next few pages will help you identify your internal network and the support people with whom you need to build relationships. Keep the above definitions in mind to ensure your network is complete.

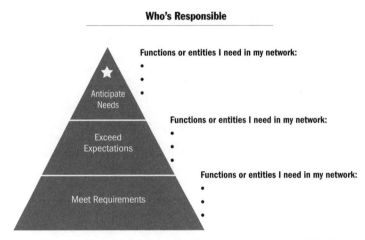

Who's Responsible

Functions or entities I need in my network:
-
-
-

Anticipate Needs

Functions or entities I need in my network:
-
-
-

Exceed Expectations

Functions or entities I need in my network:
-
-
-

Meet Requirements

Copyright © 2000, Personnel Decisions International Corporation. All Rights Reserved.

Meeting Requirements

As described, the first tier of the hierarchy is the basics in your company's value chain of product / service quality, price, on-time and complete delivery, reliability and ordering processes.

Who, then, is responsible for each of these basic components of doing business? Who do you call when something has gone wrong? This level of your internal network is generally fairly easy to define, but the importance of you recognizing its contribution to your account cannot be overemphasized.

To define who the contributors at this level are, ask yourself the following questions. Jot your thoughts on the "Who's Responsible" hierarchy above.

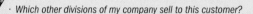

· Which other divisions of my company sell to this customer?

· What geographies (e.g., regions, countries) sell to this customer?

· Who oversees the delivery function? The order function?

· Who creates the core products or services we provide?

· Who establishes pricing and terms?

Perhaps your company is similar to one multi-national, multi-divisional company we recently worked with:

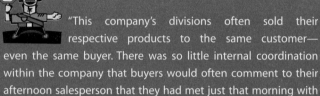

"This company's divisions often sold their respective products to the same customer—even the same buyer. There was so little internal coordination within the company that buyers would often comment to their afternoon salesperson that they had met just that morning with the salesperson from another division. Not only did the afternoon guy not know about the morning meeting, but he often did not even know who his counterpart was in that other division!"

The first thought that comes to mind in regards to this anecdote is that this company really needs to establish a strategic account management program. However, this issue would still emerge in a SAM program because SAMs especially need to know who's who and your customers need to know that someone is working to create better coordination and communications internally in your company. You'll find your own internal effectiveness increase as you help to create others' internal networks and will be viewed as one who strives to create value inside your own organization, as well as for the customer.

After defining the network of sales channels into your customer, examine the basic processes of manufacturing, ordering, delivery and invoicing. As you map these processes, identify where the supplier / customer interfaces take place and who has operational responsibility for them. As you develop your own network, aim to have at least one internal contact in every critical customer-impacting function. Although one use of these contacts is to have a go-to person should issues arise, you will realize the long-term value of these contacts when you are able to involve them in creating new solutions. In addition, you will build a deeper understanding of what is possible for your customer and how it will affect your company in turn.

Pricing is another area in which you should have a contact. Regardless of whether this function resides in marketing, product management, manufacturing or finance, you need to know who to involve when opportunities arise that require understanding different pricing scenarios. This is one area that might also require executive management approvals, so understanding the flow of how pricing decisions are made, including levels of authority, is important.

Exceeding Expectations

The next level of the relationship hierarchy is that of exceeding expectations. This includes the people with whom your customer interfaces for such needs as customer service, on-site or technical support, training and day-to-day account management.

Ask yourself the following questions to ensure a complete understanding of who contributes to this level of the hierarchy. Again, document your thoughts on the "Who's Responsible" hierarchy on page 57.

> · Who do my customers call when they have questions about our products or services? Who do users call?
>
> · Who do our customers, or the end-users, call with problems or issues?
>
> · Who follows up with customers after an installation or on-site event?

In addition to defining the functions, ensure that you have a contact in each of the critical customer-interface areas. They can be additional eyes and ears for you.

Anticipate Needs

As you think about the "anticipate and meet needs" level of the relationship hierarchy, think about the strategic goals you already have established for your account. Once again, the "Who's Responsible" hierarchy on page 57 can be used to record your thoughts.

> · What divisions or functions will be affected by my solution?
>
> · Will anyone's results be more difficult to achieve if my solution is implemented?
>
> · Who is able to approve the kinds of changes I am seeking?
>
> · Who will help me design the solution details?
>
> · Are the supporting systems or infrastructure in place?
>
> · Who typically drives the development of new product or service offerings?

These are also questions that will be asked again in Chapter 6, when you are navigating the organization with a specific outcome in mind. However, since you are thinking about your network now, it is helpful to think as broadly as possible.

How Do You Get to Know Your Internal Network?

Once you've identified who your internal network should include, you need to better understand what they do and to build relationships with them.

Your objective is to help your company break out of the win-lose mentality that some entities might view of strategic accounts in general, or of your idea in particular. You will be better prepared to create collaboration (i.e., influence through win-win) by exploring the perceptions and needs they have.

In this section, we look at each of the functions from which you are most likely to need support. If you work in a multi-national firm, and countries other than your own also sell to or service your customer, your network needs to include those countries. You will become most knowledgeable if you build your own contacts and your own understanding of your company.

We will use the term **"entity"** to mean either a **functional area**, a **country / region** or a **business unit**. Your goal is to understand the entities as they stand alone, as well as how they interrelate with others. The larger your company, the more complex you will find the interrelationships among them. In fact, you often find that it is these relationships or handoffs where you need the most insight and navigational skills.

For each entity, a worksheet is provided to guide your learning. The following are common elements of which you should develop an understanding, regardless of the group you are talking to.

- *What are the three most important goals that you are trying to achieve in the current and next fiscal year?*

- *How is success measured for you? What are your three to five most important measurements?*

- *How does your work impact my customer?*

- *How do you view my customer?*

Use the worksheets provided to guide you when you ask questions to get to know each of the entities that should be in your internal network. You can think of each worksheet as an interview guide, shaping the questions you ask that help you explore your own company. Identify those functions or countries where you have the greatest opportunities (or greatest risks).

Manufacturing

If you sell products (versus services only) to your customer, a better understanding of the manufacturing environment will enable you to more quickly recognize opportunities. It will also help you to identify challenges that your ideas create for this part of your company. Short of taking an assignment in a plant, there is generally no better way to understand this function than to regularly visit a site and walk the floor with a person you consider important in your internal network.

In addition to annual measurements, most plants also have daily and weekly goals for which they conduct detailed tracking. Because of the importance of these measurements to managers' performance ratings, you will need to understand the major factors that impact whether or not they are able to meet their goals.

You also need to understand the supply chain. How and from where are their raw materials procured? What impacts their ability to get what they need, when they need it? If there are issues with getting the materials they need, how do allocation decisions get made? How do they impact your customer? When you learn more about your company's procurement processes, you might find that you need to include procurement in your internal network. This is one of those interrelationships mentioned that might drive the need for additional fact-finding.

You should understand any impending changes in how they run their business—e.g., in procurement of materials, labor management, inventory management or other customers' demands that could impact the manufacturing area and / or your customer. Be sure you understand the issues that are being faced and how they are being analyzed. Most manufacturing organizations have greatly reduced the amount of raw material they keep on hand as well as the amount of inventory they are willing to store prior to shipment. This can impact their degree of flexibility to changing customer needs.

As with all the entities you are getting to know, develop an understanding of the key measurement areas for senior executives. When you propose ideas, anything that negatively affects their ability to meet their key measurements will require different influence strategies on your part. If they cannot remain "whole" with their boss, you will likely need to involve their senior management as part of your influence approach.

Gain an understanding of their perceptions of your customer.

You might be surprised to learn that despite how important your customer is to you, it is not even recognized at the manufacturing level. Is this a problem? If so, what could you do to change that?

It is important for you to recognize how this organization could benefit from what you know and do. For example, do they know how their outputs are used in your customer's organization? Do they know the impact it has on the customer if they do not deliver to the specifications? Have you helped them establish counterpart relationships in your customer's organization? Employees generally take more ownership of their work when they understand the impact it has on others.

Manufacturing	
Primary sites that support my customer:	Account Team Representative: Key contacts:
Organizational goals:	Annual measurement criteria: Daily / Weekly measurements:
Factors that impact their ability to meet internal goals:	Factors that impact their ability to meet my customer's requirements:
Critical source(s) of raw materials	Impending changes and challenges:
My customer's use of this organization's deliverables:	
Manufacturing's view of my customer:	
In what ways are we not aligned with each other?	What could generate better collaboration between us?
What I need to do to be better positioned in this organization:	

Field Sales

The field sales organization is perhaps the cause of more challenges, generally related to "turf", than any other function. When strategic account management programs are initiated, this is the group that sees and feels the impact most quickly. On the one hand, you are likely to have existing relationships with key contacts in the field sales organization. On the other hand, you probably can never do too much in terms of building relationships with them.

We will assume that any issues related to field sales compensation, commissions and quotas were dealt with when the strategic account management program was formed. We are not suggesting that you, as a SAM, get directly involved with these issues. However, you will find these issues are apt to surface again when you propose change, so it is important that you take time to understand how salespeople might be impacted.

Best Practice

"One of my responsibilities is to be able to bring the local sales teams out to the remote locations to meet the customer. What I bring to the sales teams is the fact that I am a world-wide account manager and I have some knowledge and expertise of the customer and the successes we have had with this customer in its entirety as well as within that line of business. What the customer sees is the best of a global presence (me) and the best of a local presence, all in the same set of meetings. Customers really respond to that approach."

As you build relationships with the field, understanding their goals and measurements is key to understanding how they will spend their time. The sales function is one where people can (and will) quickly change their priorities should their compensation or commission structure be revised. These changes have the potential to aid your cause or to create barriers to what you are trying to achieve in your account.

The issue of relationship management roles should also have been addressed when the strategic account management program was established. However, this is an area that often needs fine-tuning. Detailed discussions addressing "who does what," including both specific responsibilities and where hand-offs occur, are often critical to building solid internal relationships.

You also might run into some long-held bitter feelings about the establishment of your company's strategic account management program. When SAM programs are formed, field salespeople often feel as though something is being taken away from them. This may or may not be true, but it's often the perception. As one SAMA board member related:

"When our corporate account managers were introduced, we felt like they were greeted with 'Who are you and what are you doing here?'"

When a strategic account program is established with the idea of "adding to" what is currently accomplished, it makes it easier to communicate the importance of already-established roles and processes—especially in the field sales organization. I.e., you as a SAM endeavor to "add to" the overall relationship by establishing relationships at levels that were not previously there and creating solutions that would not have otherwise emerged. Since you are often being faced with the concern that you are "taking something" away from the salespeople you are meeting with, anything you can do to emphasize your role of "adding to" will help.

As you build your relationships, be aware that hard feelings do not go away quickly. Even if your SAM program was formed long before you started in your position, there could still be lingering negative attitudes.

In a well-structured strategic account management program, the SAM will have an ongoing working relationship with each of the salespeople integral to account success. If you do not also have a relationship with someone at the sales management level, you need to develop one. Having a liaison who can share strategy with you, help you understand the impact of future change and be an advocate for you when needed is important groundwork to lay.

Think, too, in terms of finding out what kinds of information the salespeople need more of. As mentioned in Chapter 3, open communications are critical to the building of trust. Ask how you can best keep them informed of:

- The status of corporate agreements you are pursuing or have signed;
- Market intelligence or competitive information;
- Changes in your customer's management or decision-making hierarchy;
- Future changes in product or service needs;
- Pricing changes;
- Anticipated backlogs or surpluses;

- Distribution issues; and

- Effects of regulatory or environmental changes.

Field Sales	
Primary divisions / geographies that sell to my customer, and relative importance of my customer to them: *Division / Geography* *Importance*	Account Team Representative: Key contacts:
Organizational goals:	Key measurement criteria that impact compensation: Other measurement criteria:
How they contribute to success in my account:	How my customer contributes to their success: Factors in this customer that hinder their success:
Their view of my customer:	
Changes / challenges this organization faces in the future:	
In what ways are we not aligned with each other?	What could generate better collaboration between us?
What I need to do to be better positioned in this organization:	

Customer Service / Technical Support

The customer service area is one that often surprises even the most knowledgeable SAM. This is an organization that can give you some of the richest and most timely feedback about what customers like and dislike about your company's products and services. If you have never done it, you will be amazed at how much can be learned in half a day of observing calls or monitoring e-mail requests for help.

Due to its direct customer contact, this is also a group that takes pride in its dedication to customers. Whereas some functional areas in your company need to be educated on what being customer-focused means (see also Chapter 5), this is one that should be more than able to teach it.

On the less positive side, policies and procedures often are developed within this organization with minimal understanding of their impact on the customer. Understanding how policies and procedures get developed is critical. For example, while customer service can work more efficiently by allowing any representative to take any call, strategic account contacts would often feel better served if they had a core team servicing them. Involving customer service directly with your account allows your customer's needs to be more uniquely represented.

As with other functions, understanding how the group is measured is also key to understanding how the service your customer receives might be impacted by internal priorities. Like manufacturing, customer service has daily goals that are tracked and highly visible, and some of these goals are in conflict with the definition of "excellent customer service." If keeping call time to a minimum is a key measurement area, representatives might resist asking for other issues or problems the customer might be experiencing. When customer service is short-staffed, additional pressure to keep call time to a minimum will be felt. Your customer, however, wants more attention.

You also might hear frustrations from the associates with whom you speak. They just cannot understand why the company won't make certain changes that would clearly make the customers happier. Recognize that it's possible they are hearing from (hopefully) a small segment of customers who are having this issue, even though a large percentage of that small segment is calling in about it. You can help them gain perspective on whether this is a problem that impacts a large number of customers, or simply a small number of customers who are vocal about it. Also recognize, however, that this kind of feedback could be an early warning of a real problem. This front-line function is often the first to hear, and having a close link to this feedback will help you to become aware of emerging issues and then to size up their magnitude.

Technical support has been grouped in with customer service for a couple of reasons. First, in many companies a separate technical support function is not needed. Second, the two functions are similarly structured and managed, although there is likely more training needed and a higher expectation from customers for the technical support function. If the functions are separate, simply use two worksheets. You will need to develop two sets of contacts and relationships as well.

Customer Service / Technical Support	
Locations that service my customer:	Account Team Representative: Key Contacts:
Organizational goals:	Annual measurement criteria: Daily / weekly measurements:
How they are structured to service my customer:	How they contribute to success in my customer:
Their view of my customer:	
Their view of what is needed to increase customer satisfaction:	
In what ways are we not aligned with each other?	What could generate better collaboration between us?
What I need to do to be better positioned in this organization:	

Global Entities

When a customer is sold to, or serviced by, multiple countries within your company, complexities will exist.

Your company may have country-specific account managers, and may or may not have a coordinated selling approach. Much depends on the structure of your strategic account program. Whether or not you are a SAM with global responsibilities, you should first determine who else has account management responsibilities for your customer. And if you have global responsibilities, there is likely much about the other countries and their relationship with your customer that you do not fully understand.

If your company is traditionally structured, each country likely has a senior executive who has profit-and-loss responsibility, similar to the multiple business units of the corporation. An implication of this is that as different countries sell to their customers, the number of dimensions around which there is internal financial interest increases. Not only is each country looking at its sales (and profits, if available) by customer, but each business unit is also tracking its numbers, as are the global account managers. What might make financial sense to a global SAM could have wildly varying reactions from various countries. In addition, the issue of control – totally separate from financials – is apt to get in the way of rational conversation and decision-making.

It is important that the SAM understand the stakes of each country's management team that currently sells, or could sell, to your account. Finding someone who can coach you on local business practices, intra-company politics and the culture and laws of each country will help you get better grounded. Find out what makes a good impression and what you should be certain to avoid.

Our Survey Says...

The Major Difficulties Experienced by Global Account Managers Responding to the Survey Were Identified, in Order of Importance, as:

Difficulty	Percentage
Global / local conflicts of interest	68%
Regional / local implementation of global strategies	61%
Lack of an integrated IT system	50%
Managing & coordinating multi-national teams	44%
Demands of the customer exceed local capability	25%
Language difficulties	24%
Regional / local players damage global relationship	21%
Local capability exceeds global capability	20%

Source: 2000, Study of Global Account Management Practices, SAMA, The Sales Research Trust.

As part of your strategy to build strong internal relationships, include representatives from key geographies as you develop a global vision for your account. The more you can make their goals part of your goal, the more likely your actions will be aligned. More alignment means less frustration.

Use the following worksheet for each country that plays a role in your account. Should there be a long list of those countries, prioritize based on the importance of your customer to that country's success.

Country / Region:	
Products / services this country sells to my account:	Account Team Representative:
	Key contacts:
My customer's percentage (or rank) of this country's sales:	Key senior management contacts:
Country's goals:	Key measurement criteria:
Where the sales and support functions (relevant to my account) are located:	
Changes / challenges the country faces in the future:	This country's view of my customer:
What advantages, and disadvantages, does this country offer to my customer?	
What is unique about the competitive landscape in this country / region?	
In what ways are we aligned with each other? What is working well?	
In what ways are we not aligned with each other?	What could generate better collaboration between us?
What I need to do to be better positioned with our company in this country / region:	

Product Development

When SAMs have an idea that needs to be studied and refined, they know the value of going to product development for help. What SAMs do not always understand is that by establishing relationships with the product development function, they build their own capability to proactively offer more ideas to their customer. Product development can be a strategic ally, identifying opportunities you might not have otherwise seen.

Product developers explore ways to improve current products as well as new ones. In fact, they often feel their own frustrations when they find themselves with the proverbial "innovative solution in search of a problem." Sharing customer ideas and needs with the product developers helps them be more closely aligned with what customers need.

Keeping informed of improvements product developers are studying, or new products they are designing, lets your customer know you are innovating and improving. You can also learn useful information that can serve as value-add to your customer. For example, if you share with the product developers that your customer is moving in a particular direction, this guides them to sharing with you pertinent information they might not have realized you needed.

You should also help to orchestrate linkages between product development and its counterparts in your customer organization. If your customer uses your products in its manufacturing process, its product developers are likely relaying to their procurement organization the specifications for components or ingredients to be sourced. Meanwhile, your developers might be patenting various processes that produce a product with unique characteristics. By creating a relationship between your developers and your customer's, you increase the potential of your unique product achieving the status of preferred product.

By establishing an ongoing relationship with your product developers, you also have easier access to their ideas when you are trying to formulate a solution for your customer. Most SAMs can't possibly understand the details of all the products their company provides. It is more important to understand the needs customers have and to have a vision of how your company could help meet those needs, and then utilize internal resources to work out the details of exactly what the solution will look like.

Use the following as a guide to explore how best to work with the product developers in your company.

Product Development	
Primary groups that support my customer:	Account Team Representative: Key contacts:
Organizational goals:	Key measurement criteria:
Initiatives underway that might benefit my customer:	
Changes / Challenges product development faces in the future:	
What they are hearing other customers ask for:	Their view of my customer:
In what ways are we not aligned with each other?	What could generate better collaboration between us?
What I need to do to be better positioned in this organization:	

Information Technology (IT)

Depending on the products or services you sell, this function might already be an integral part of your team. Much depends on whether IT is the product (or integral part of the product) you sell, a delivery mechanism, a competitive differentiator or an unseen part of the infrastructure. Even if IT professionals are not perceived to play a strategic role, it is worth understanding the role that they play and determining if their contributions can (or should) be expanded.

IT groups differ. Some are highly strategic and very attuned to business and customer needs; they work hard to partner with parts of the business. Others, however, are slow to change. They operate in a "receive mode"—i.e., they wait until requests are made and needs are expressed, versus proactively learning about their internal customers' needs and priorities. When they do get involved in a more proactive manner, there are inevitably areas in which they can add value immediately. These can be both in customer-affecting areas and building internal efficiencies.

IT also is an area that has likely been affected by cost-cutting. After organizational expansion in the late 1990s due to Y2K and dot-com fervor, IT departments experienced deep cuts, or even complete outsourcing. IT leaders are asked to justify their initiatives more often than in the past, so they are less likely to offer anything "nice but not necessary." Technology has lost some of the glitter, and in some companies it is seen only as supporting strategy, not leading it.

Learn how the IT function currently impacts your customer. Does it play a significant visible role, or is it an underlying support role? How might their role change in the next two years?

What are your customers asking for in the area of technology, and how is that being communicated to your IT professionals? This is an area in which many resources can be expended and still not meet the real need of the customer. Recognizing *why* customers are asking for a technology change or enhancement, not simply *what* they are asking is key to using IT resources appropriately.

In addition to its role with your customer, IT might also play an internal support role—e.g., helping your internal account team or contacts stay better informed. There are a myriad of ways they can do this, and not all of them are cost-prohibitive. Simply establishing an account site within your company's intranet and including a directory of documents is a first step to enhanced knowledge and communications. The SAM organization will likely want to develop a more sophisticated structure at some point, but creating a short-term solution can be a wise investment. If your company does implement a customer relationship management (CRM) system, be sure your strategic account managers are represented in the planning phase. Many a CRM system has been built with less-than-desired results for SAMs, and one reason is that the planning phase did not include them.

Information Technology (IT)	
Primary groups that support my customer:	Account Team Representative: Key contacts:
Organizational goals:	Key measurement criteria:
How IT supports my account:	
Changes / Challenges IT faces in the future:	
What IT is hearing other customers ask for:	IT's view of my customer:
In what ways are we not aligned with each other?	What could generate better collaboration between us?
What I need to do to be better positioned in this organization:	

Human Resources (HR)

HR, you say? Why?

Unfortunately, many SAMs view their HR department as only a resource for hiring or firing purposes. The lack of partnering between these two groups was visibly apparent at SAMA's 2002 Executive Leadership Symposium, attended by about 75 directors of strategic account programs.

> *When one speaker asked how many of the attendees had*
> *a good working relationship with their human resources*
> *department, not one person raised their hand.*

In fact, many HR organizations today are rightfully seated at the strategy table with key line executives. Companies that understand the critical importance of talent management know that a human resources function that is purely reactionary will not deliver the talent that is needed for the corporation's future success. Effective HR organizations have moved beyond delivering requested services to being able to help drive strategy, based on understanding the talent implications of that strategy.

There are several ways that a contact in HR can help you. To the extent that your vision of a customer solution has people-related consequences, a knowledgeable HR contact can help you define any limitations you might face. This could be a skills limitation, or it might involve labor relations. Gaining some level of understanding of these implications from someone who is not directly involved, and therefore likely to be less emotional about the topic, will prepare you for other meetings.

If HR is not well acquainted with your strategic accounts organization, make the first move. When HR understands what you are trying to achieve, it will also better understand the impact of conflicting goals and measures. For example, it might not have understood the importance of appropriate compensation plans for the field sales organization relative to strategic accounts.

Another way that HR can help you is with your own professional success. For example, are you struggling with leading your account team? Would a facilitator help your meetings be more effective? Many SAMs do not realize that internal resources might be available to help them gain needed skills. Or perhaps the "rules" on training budgets need to be revised, to fund more training for the high-impact position of SAM.

The fact that HR is striving to build an internal network of its own makes it valuable to you as you strive to build yours. As HR moved from just delivering the basics of "hiring and firing", it likely began to approach the functional areas and various geographies as customers of its own. HR generalists might be able to share with you important insights about some of the entities you are seeking to better understand. You will find that HR professionals are often well networked throughout the organization, and they may in fact provide you with some of the introductions you want.

They also can become ambassadors for your SAM program by advocating the benefits / rewards of what you are trying to achieve. This can be helpful both in obtaining the buy-in you need for certain initiatives, as well as generating interest in the SAM position as a potential career for young talent.

Human Resources (HR)	
How HR supports our strategic accounts program:	Key contacts:
Organizational goals:	Key measurement criteria:
Changes / Challenges HR faces in the future:	
How HR supports the functions / geographies critical to my internal network:	
In what ways are we not aligned with each other?	What could generate better collaboration between us?
How does / could HR contribute to my professional success?	
What I need to do to better utilize Human Resources:	

Marketing

The role of marketing varies widely, so understanding its charter is the first step to recognizing the value it can provide. For example, in most consumer products companies, the marketing function speaks primarily to the consumer through various forms of advertising, even though the company sells only through retailers or distributors. In some manufacturing companies, you might find the marketing organization does little more than design collateral carried by the salespeople. Whatever its activities, it will have ideas and contacts you should learn about.

Most marketing organizations conduct studies of the competitive landscape and industry trends. Be sure to keep up-to-date on the work they are doing. This, in fact, is an easy ice-breaker for you as you work to build relationships with that function—they love to talk about analysis they have done. This information is useful when talking to your customer as well. Sharing research findings is part of the value-add you can offer, and you can then segue into a discussion about opportunities the findings suggest.

In marketing organizations that run advertising campaigns and / or design promotions, a calendar of the coming year's activities is established well in advance, locking in budget dollars. Although this might seem to be a barrier to new ideas you have, there is typically someone who can override budget constraints—assuming you have credible evidence of the benefits of doing so.

Marketing can help you gather such evidence as well. Whether it is research it already has, or a focus group or other research it designs specifically to get input on your subject of interest, ask for help in this area.

Do Marketing Team Members Regularly Accompany the Sales Force on Sales Calls?

Definitely No	58%
Sometimes	27%
Definitely Yes	15%

Source: 2002, Marketing Alignment Research Study, SAMA, Revenue Storm.

Marketing professionals also tend to be great for networking. Are you having trouble getting in to see your account's marketing director? Offer to bring *your* company's marketing director with you; you will be surprised how quickly doors will open. The purpose of bringing the two directors together is to explore how your company's marketing plans might be able to support your customer's plans. During the meeting, you will expand your customer network and learn what information you were seeking in the first place.

As with many functions, simply talking about your respective jobs is apt to generate ideas on how you can work more collaboratively with each other. This is a functional area that has a limited number of people in its department, so whatever you can do to elevate the needs of your customer or of strategic accounts in general will likely help you at some point in the future.

Marketing	
How marketing supports my customer:	Account Team Representative:
	Key contacts:
Organizational goals:	Key measurement criteria:
Budgets / marketing calendar established by (dates):	
Lead times needed for various activities:	
The role they see for themselves with my account (or strategic accounts in general):	Marketing's view of my customer:
Marketing's contacts that could be useful to my account:	
In what ways are we not aligned with each other?	What could generate better collaboration between us?
What I need to do to be better positioned in this organization:	

Group Learning

As a SAM, you need to build your own network of relationships, as outlined in this chapter. If you are one in a group of SAMs, however, your group should consider leveraging your collective time, as well as the time of some of your contacts, for group learning.

Whereas relationships need to be built one by one, learning about a function's priorities can be done as a group. Ask a functional representative to come into a SAM meeting and talk about the subjects we outlined in the templates. Or see if a group of you can visit a site together, thus asking for one tour instead of several.

Remember,

In this step, you are in a "learn and absorb" mode.

You are building relationships and your knowledge base so they are there when you need them. Don't take either for granted!

Summary

We've just outlined numerous ideas for building your internal network by first better understanding it. As we stated at the very beginning of this chapter, many of these tools parallel strategies that you already employ when you sell to the external customer. You actually have more tools at your disposal when you approach internal selling in a methodical manner (e.g., access to private company information, access to sites and an internal network that can facilitate access to individuals you need to meet with), which you might say is a good thing, given how difficult the internal sell can be.

Complete the quick action plan below, and proceed to the next chapter where another powerful tool is at your disposal—the customer.

My vision:
Five years from now, I would like my customer to say the following about the collaboration he sees in our company:

"

"

To make this happen, I need to learn more about:

I also need to be doing more of:

Chapter 5:
Create Customer Advocates

Customers expect their strategic account manager to be their advocate, and in fact many SAM job descriptions have the responsibility of "customer advocacy" described in detail. Being a customer advocate can be difficult when the rest of the organization does not feel the same ownership for supporting the customer as you do. Or perhaps they feel they are supporting the customer, and "It's just all those changes you're seeking that are the problem. After all, things have worked just fine in the past, and the customer does a lot of business with us, so why do we need to do something different now?"

The SAM has internalized things that the rest of the organization hasn't had the same opportunity to experience. The insights gained from spending time with customers, visiting their locations, seeing their pain and walking side-by-side with them helps create the passion for the customer that great SAMs bring to their job. But the SAM's passion will not be enough.

Part of your job is to help others relate to the customer. That is what this chapter will help you do.

We'll start with a self-test. Use it as a guide to the steps that you can take to ensure you are contributing to a culture of customer advocacy in your company.

> "You've got to come back to your company and get the resources, whether they be manufacturing, operations or finance, to support what the customer needs, and unfortunately a lot of these people have very limited backgrounds or appreciation of customer-focus. The majority of people that you get support from in a global account environment have never even been in that country, so how in the heck are they going to relate to the Argentinean market and what goes on there?"

	Strongly Disagree 1 - - - - 2 - - - - 3 - - - - 4 - - - - 5	Somewhat Agree	Strongly Agree
1. I continually look for ways to get my customer in front of non-sales people in my company.	1 - - - - - 2 - - - - - 3 - - - - - 4 - - - - - 5		
2. I have organized visits for employees from my company to go to my customer's location.	1 - - - - - 2 - - - - - 3 - - - - - 4 - - - - - 5		
3. I help to create linkages between my customer and the senior executives of my company.	1 - - - - - 2 - - - - - 3 - - - - - 4 - - - - - 5		
4. My company proactively seeks customer input on future products and services we might offer.	1 - - - - - 2 - - - - - 3 - - - - - 4 - - - - - 5		
5. When I involve senior management with my account in a peer-to-peer meeting, I brief them on our objectives in advance, and we establish our respective roles.	1 - - - - - 2 - - - - - 3 - - - - - 4 - - - - - 5		
6. Members of my account team understand the needs of their counterparts in the customer organization.	1 - - - - - 2 - - - - - 3 - - - - - 4 - - - - - 5		
7. The feedback we get from customers is specific enough that we understand how to take appropriate action.	1 - - - - - 2 - - - - - 3 - - - - - 4 - - - - - 5		
8. Employees whose work impacts my customer know who our strategic accounts are and their importance to our business.	1 - - - - - 2 - - - - - 3 - - - - - 4 - - - - - 5		
9. Members of my account team share a common view on how our company could best serve the customer.	1 - - - - - 2 - - - - - 3 - - - - - 4 - - - - - 5		

Make the Customer Real

When Frank Lloyd Wright designed his famous houses, the large windows were, in his words, meant to "bring the outside in."

Similarly, your goal is to bring your customer in. Sometimes you will do this literally, other times you will be its representative in your company and other times, you'll take your organization to the customer to make it happen.

In this chapter we will discuss the strategy of orchestrating for others in your company some of the same experiences that you have had. We call this "making the customer real" to the rest of the organization. The more real you can make the customer, the easier it is to influence internally. When employees in the various silos truly know the customer – versus just learning about the customer through second or third-hand information – they are more likely to embrace the customer's needs and, in turn, embrace the SAM's strategy. They become an extension of the SAM's voice, which helps leverage the SAM's time and energy.

There are many ways to accomplish "making the customer real," and all of the approaches have the same objective in mind:

Help others in the organization walk in your customer's shoes. They will be more likely to develop the same passion for change that you have developed. When they become customer advocates, your job is made much easier.

The How-To's

The approaches we describe take time, so they should be a part of your long-term strategy as a SAM. When the time comes that you need to influence internally, it will likely be too late to implement the ideas in this chapter if you have not already built these foundations. Assume you are going to need to influence others at some point, and build your base of customer advocates now.

Customer Collateral

Obtaining collateral from your customer is a good starting point, but even more powerful is asking how your customer orients its new employees. One Marriott account manager, in order to gain a deeper understanding of his customer's business and industry, attended its new employee orientation session. Often such sessions include a video that your customer would be willing to let you borrow for use with the employees in your company who support them. It's a great tool for you to use internally. Everyone, from your account team members to the associates who handle returns, will feel a bit closer to the customer after they've seen it.

A customer "wall of fame" is also a means to enhance visibility. Assuming it is OK with your customers to do so, display their logos in a prominent place, so employees see who uses your products or services. Better yet, display products (or pictures of them) that use

"It really is a matter of managing communications and relationships between people within your own company, yourself and the customer. You constantly have to be marketing internally that these customers are the future of your company. You have to be making sure that the various functional groups understand the importance of certain customers to the future of the company and to their future."

Director Strategic Accounts, U.S.-based Fortune 500 Chemical Company

your components. When you visit employees, tell a story of the path that raw materials take through your company, how your product gets to the customer and how it becomes part of the customer's final product. If you're a service company, you can do the same thing. Describe who does what, and how.

Internal Newsletters

Either your company, or each division within your company, has monthly or quarterly employee newsletters. This is another opportunity for you to bring visibility to your customer, and to customers in general.

Like company collateral, however, this is a passive approach that is dependent on the reader to take action (in this case, read the article). You can put information in front of others, but you cannot control whether they will take the time to notice it. In general, a "facts" article about when your customer's company was founded, how many employees it has and what its primary businesses are is very "blah" to many of your potential readers. In order to draw the attention of your readers, write from a perspective they will more easily relate to.

Bring the reader's own organization into the article. One way you can do that is to use numbers that will "wow" the reader:

- *Do you know how many widgets we shipped to Y-Corp last year? 27 million!*

- *If we lined up all the users of our – [fill in your product or service here] – they would fill the convention center ten times!*

- *The ingredients we shipped to Z-Foods were used to make enough potato chips to give every household in our country ten bags!*

This is also an opportunity to recognize an entire work group, a function or individual employees. Use quotes from the customer, which reflect good work that has been done by these groups, and the benefits that your customer received from their efforts (increased sales or retention of an account, for instance). Describe how they are the heroes.

Customer Panels

Various organizations within your company have periodic all-employee meetings, and they are often looking to include a motivational speaker or group learning experience as a part of it. A powerful addition to any such meeting is to bring in a few customers to serve on a panel. It is incredible how the level of customer focus – even in organizations whose employees interact with customers on the telephone, such as customer service or technical support – will increase after sitting face-to-face with the customer. In addition, it reinforces to the customers who serve on the panel (or might later read about it in a customer newsletter) that your company is listening.

If you have the opportunity to help organize such an event, think of the objectives you want to achieve in advance. For example, you may want to strengthen the organization's readiness prior to new product introductions. Or perhaps the length of time customers spend explaining the history of their issue is a problem when they have to make repeat calls. Thinking through what you want to accomplish will help you to select the appropriate customers and prepare them in advance.

The panel should be introduced by one of the organization's executives, or by a SAM who is managing a relationship with one of the customers. Begin with a brief (ten minute) presentation. This presentation will describe the importance of customer focus. Perhaps you can include a description of your company's strategies toward managing customer relationships, linking customer focus with values or goals that the organization has publicly stated are critical to success. The introduction should create a foundation from which the customer panel will provide its insights.

The customer panel will follow. You'll need to have a moderator for the panel. Consider using someone who has experience doing this, as you want the moderator to remain objective throughout the session. The moderator will ask each panelist to describe the nature

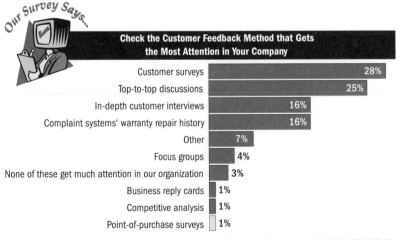

Check the Customer Feedback Method that Gets the Most Attention in Your Company

Customer surveys	28%
Top-to-top discussions	25%
In-depth customer interviews	16%
Complaint systems' warranty repair history	16%
Other	7%
Focus groups	4%
None of these get much attention in our organization	3%
Business reply cards	1%
Competitive analysis	1%
Point-of-purchase surveys	1%

Source: 2001, Survey on Leading-Edge Practices for Measuring & Managing Customer Loyalty, SAMA, PDI, IMPAX.

of their company's relationship with your company. Then, a series of questions will be posed to the panel.

Design questions that are relevant to the audience. They might include such topics as:

- *How have your needs, related to the products / services you receive from this company, changed over the past few years?*

- *What is the most important thing that you look for in a supplier (in this industry)?*

- *When have you been 'WOWed' by a supplier? Why?*

- *When have you been 'WOWed' by us? Why?*

- *What causes you to be disappointed in a supplier?*

- *What differentiates our company from our competitors? (Both positive and negative comparisons should be elicited.)*

Share the questions in advance with your customers so they have time to think about their responses. Encourage them to be candid; everyone will benefit if constructive criticism is provided along with praise.

In addition to the prepared questions, time should be allotted for the audience to ask their own questions of any or all of the participants. Just in case the audience is a bit shy at first, you should also be prepared with some questions of your own.

Throughout the panel discussion, be sure that someone is taking detailed notes. The notes can be used to write an article for your internal company newsletter, or to distribute back to the organization to reinforce the customers' key points. Incorporate some of the comments into new employees' initial training. New employees get so much information on product, process and procedures thrown at them—but it's the customer stories that will be remembered most vividly, especially if you can use a video or audiotape.

Hearing customers speak on a panel is a powerful experience for employees. This can be especially so for those employees whose functional orientation causes them to view customers from a fairly narrow perspective. In addition, customers appreciate the enthusiasm they see in the audience. They recognize that you support a customer-focused culture when you sponsor such an event.

Site Visits

If possible, arrange for employees of your company to visit customer sites. Start with your core account team, since they are the people who you most need to feel connected with the customer.

Let your customer know that you'd like to take your team onsite to have a two day (or whatever) planning meeting, and as part of that meeting you would like everyone to get a tour and have a chance to talk to some of the users of your products and services. They will probably be more than willing to find you meeting space and arrange for the activities you have planned.

In addition to your account team, consider other employees who might not interact directly with customers. Seeing how customers use your products and services can be an especially meaningful experience for them. While you can usually justify members of an account team traveling to a customer location, you might have to get more creative to get some of the "back office" or line employees out for a visit.

The easiest visit to arrange is when you are fortunate enough to have a group of employees who work within easy travel distance of a major customer facility. Reminiscent of "field trip" days, the employees will enjoy the trip, but more importantly, will internalize how their work impacts the customer. Even snafus can work to your advantage. How will the shipping people feel if they see damaged cartons unloaded on the delivery dock? Or if manufacturing employees see what kinds of paperwork have to be completed for damaged parts?

More feasible and cost-effective than shuttling a work group on a field trip is to have just a few delegates travel to the customer site. Employees could be chosen for this trip as recognition for job performance, or simply chosen by their peers. In return for the trip they will be asked to attend group meetings to share with their peers what they learned. In addition to creating customer advocates out of the individuals who visited the site, you will then be using them to help influence their peers for you.

The following are questions that employees who visit a customer site should seek answers to on their visit:

- *How does our customer use our products (or services)?*

- *How important are our products (or services) to what our customer does?*

- *What does the customer like, or appreciate, most about our products and services?*

- *What impact does it have on our customer when it doesn't get from us what it needs?*

- *What are the most important things that our company can do to ensure everything goes smoothly for the customer?*

Leading an Account Team

We've made several references to account teams in this and previous chapters, and you may or may not be leading a formal team. It is always easiest if account teams have been formally established to support a strategic customer, versus informally calling on other functions for support of the strategic account. In fact, although we have not conducted formal research to confirm the reasons behind this, it appears that the companies that establish formal account teams are also the companies in which it is easier for SAMs to navigate internally. This trend is probably the product of a combination of cross-functional resources being easier to access, as well as formal teams being evidence of the strong senior management support that is in place.

If you are leading a cross-functional account team, you most likely face challenges. For example, either you've not led people in the past, or those who you *have* led reported to you directly. On a cross-functional account team, the time you are asking team members to spend on your account may be, in their minds (or that of their bosses), "extra" time that they really do not have available.

It is in your best interests to be effective at leading your team. In terms of your ability to influence internally, a committed account team can be a huge advantage. Team members become customer advocates as well as direct links into the parts of your company from which you will need to gain buy-in for your ideas.

PDI's TeamWise® Success Model portrays the components of effective teams. As your team's leader, develop an understanding

> "When you've got the collaboration of a strong team that is working well together with very clear and strong communication channels, then you can make all this come together. But you've got to have that trust base or that collaboration base in order to break down the traditional barriers."

PDI's TeamWise® Success Model

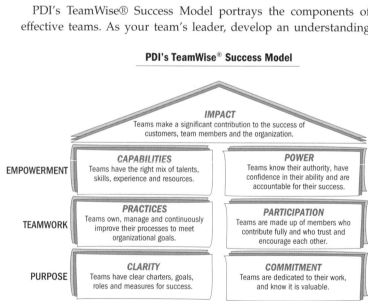

Copyright © 1999, Personnel Decisions International Corporation. All Rights Reserved.

of these components and of the suggestions we've made to help you leverage this important resource.

Purpose

"Purpose" is the foundation on which team development and performance must be built. It consists of:

- Clarity, the extent to which all members of the team understand the results the team is accountable for; and

- Commitment, the extent to which team members feel a sense of personal investment in achieving those results.

The importance of *clarity* of team purpose cannot be underestimated. It has implications for determining who should participate on the team, and it helps the team have focus from the start. Some of the questions that you should answer, or jointly explore with your team, include the following:

- *What is the scope of the opportunity with this customer?*

- *What specifically will the team be responsible for doing?*

- *What problem, issue or opportunity will be resolved if the team is successful?*

- *How will success be measured? What happens if the team is successful? Or if it is not?*

Clarity alone is not enough. Team members must also have *commitment*. Members of a cross-functional team have numerous other responsibilities. To spend the time and energy needed to support the team requires commitment, or activities related to the team will be assigned a lower priority. If some team members are not committed, it will have a negative impact on other members of the team.

Commitment is a principal challenge of any new account team, and an ongoing challenge for a globally distributed one. Yet commitment makes all the difference. We have seen commitment so high among team members that they accept smaller deals (and commissions) in their respective countries in support of the overall sale because they recognize the longer-term or broader benefits.

Generating commitment requires the team leader and sponsor to have finely tuned leadership skills. Commitment cannot be assigned via e-mail! Selling the need for organizational focus on the customer, and the initiative under development by the team, is one more component of the "internal sell." The most important questions that, when answered, will encourage team members to be committed are:

- *How will I benefit by working on the team (i.e., "What's in it for me?")?*

- *Is my senior management committed?*

Teamwork

Teamwork is defined as the ability of individual group members to work with one another in an effective and productive manner.

Team *practices* help members know their own responsibilities as well as what everyone else is doing. The SAM should work with the team to define practices that describe how team members will:

- Communicate with each other;

- Communicate with you;

- Resolve differences of opinion;

- Know what their responsibility – and others' – is;

- Escalate: When and to whom;

- Hold members accountable; and

- Measure the team's progress.

Participation refers to the interpersonal relationships among members of the team. In many cross-functional teams, this can be a particularly difficult aspect to cultivate due to the geographic dispersion of members, cultural differences, functional differences and complexity of the task. Although it can be logistically difficult, meeting at least once face-to-face can create huge benefits: people who know each other find it easier to want to work together. The more that interpersonal relationships are nurtured, the stronger the foundation will be when cooperation is most needed. Strong, balanced team participation is a measure of trust, which is an outcome of a well-led team.

Fostering participation can also happen through:

- Establishing expectations among the team members in the areas of collaboration, compromise, respect, truthfulness and openness;

- Frequent conference calls, especially at the start of your team's formation, to encourage collaboration;

- Awareness and flexible responsiveness in scheduling conference calls and meeting locations to accommodate global geography;

- Smaller sub-committee groups and corresponding calls; and

- Addressing conflict through defined processes (see Practices).

Empowerment

The basic principle behind empowerment is simple: individuals have the capacity, and are given the authority, to make decisions. They are able to take action regarding work for which they are accountable.

A necessary foundation for empowerment is that of *capabilities*. Team members need to have the necessary skills and resources to get the job done, or empowerment will not happen. When a team first forms, the required resources are defined in order to bring the right members together. As the team's purpose is further clarified, however, more knowledge often leads to the need to acquire different or additional skills and capabilities. It is important that the team always be viewed, both within and from the outside, as having the people it needs to accomplish its purpose. To the extent that your team does not have the membership it needs to accomplish its goals, you will need to seek additional resources.

Typically, teams develop two circles of membership (and influence): core and extended. Core team members (often numbering six to ten) participate regularly in team meetings and conference calls. Extended members participate episodically, or on an as-needed basis. Quarterly updates, newsletters or conference calls are sometimes used to update and re-engage global extended team members.

The second component is *power*, or the authority and discretion to act within prescribed guidelines. Team members need to have the confidence that they can take some level of action on behalf of their own organization. If they are not given the power to do so, both you and your team members will become quite frustrated. The unfortunate consequence is that you, as team leader, will be missing out on the advantages of having a team in the first place.

Using the TeamWise® Framework

Because you want your team to be an extension of you in customer advocacy, you need to do all you can to ensure the six components just discussed are in place. Team members who have a clear understanding of goals and are committed to them and your team will also be effective advocates. One SAMA member describes how his account team matured:

"There's a value to cross-pollinating the account team so it sees both sides of the equation. We identified a trust and communications factor in the breakdowns we have. In my job, I call on customer headquarters and someone else has the remote location in another country. Often, I will travel to the remote location to pave the way. We also need to bring the remote sales rep back to headquarters and let him see the other side. This can replace the situation where headquarters acts like

it is in charge and sets the strategy, and the remote team argues 'You don't understand; I live there, I know what's going on.' We should exist to serve our customer, and getting shot at in the cross-fire probably isn't the most productive thing to do."

Another way to guide your team members to becoming customer advocates is to help them proactively manage cross-functional relationships. Many may already be doing this, but typically there is room to grow in this area. The following process will help you engage your team with the customer and generate even more opportunities for growth.

Develop Strong Cross-Functional Relationships

It is a well-defined concept: create multiple relationships between your organization and the customer organization. In addition to the account manager managing relationships with key buyers, help your team build relationships from your operations to their operations, including manufacturer to manufacturer; distribution to receiving; IT to IT; R&D to product development. Why is this important? Again, the more that others interact directly with the customer, the more you can create in them a passion for serving the customer. It will then be easier for you to work through them when you seek change or growth in the relationship.

When we talk about "building relationships", we're referring primarily to the business relationship. Although the personal relationship – usually built through meals out, attending sporting events and having casual conversations – is important, establishing a business relationship is critical to doing business on a long-term basis.

Most SAMs and salespeople understand how to do this, but how do you guide employees who have not traditionally or proactively interacted with customers to "manage a relationship?" Think about your own first steps in managing a customer relationship.

1. You work to understand the customer's business environment and needs.

2. You then respond to requests, issues or opportunities that they might have, and you interact periodically to communicate information that would be of interest.

3. You also try to think ahead and to be proactive with the customer.

A tool for helping account teams manage relationships is PDI's Customer Review™ process. It consists of three steps:

Discovery	Action	Experience
Determine what is important to the customer and what issues or opportunities there are in the relationship.	Take action to address: · Issues · Opportunities Involve others, or escalate, as necessary.	As you communicate the actions taken and planned, the customer experiences enhanced service. In addition, the employees experience a deeper relationship with their key contact.

Discovery

The easiest way to develop a relationship with someone is to ask questions. That's just what you were doing throughout Chapter 4! Creating a template for your team members that outlines the kinds of questions to ask of their customers will provide them with a practice that is both easy and powerful. It's easy, because they won't have to think very hard about the kinds of things they should be learning from their new contact, and it's powerful because they will hear "the voice of the customer" directly—i.e., no filters.

Think of discovery as an interview process. There are two areas of need you and your account team members should address:

1. Current Performance: Questions related to the products and services you currently provide.

2. Future Needs: Questions that help you understand the customer's organization, challenges and future needs.

As you develop the questions related to the products and services you provide, think first about the major areas that impact the customer's view of you. Topic areas that are often included in discovery interviews include:

- Product (or service) quality;
- Communications;
- Ease of doing business;
- Understanding customer needs; and
- Value.

For each of these topic areas, your team members are seeking individualized feedback from the contacts they have been assigned. They will conduct their discovery interviews with just one customer contact at a time because it is only through understanding an individual's unique perspectives and needs that you can manage a relationship effectively.

What if you don't have an account team? There are functional employees whose work directly impacts the customer. Even if you have not established a formal mapping of employees to customers, consider having someone accompany you as you conduct discovery interviews with your contacts. For example, if you know that technology is an issue with your customer, talk with a manager from IT to see if he would be interested in joining you as you conduct a discovery interview with that contact.

Since these topic areas are related to current performance, the kinds of questions that are asked about each of them include:

- *To what degree are we meeting your requirements in this area?*

- *What should we improve?*

- *What do we do well?*

- *How do we compare to our competitors?*

- *Who does it better, and why?*

Each individual interviewed responds from his own perspective, which is how each team member's ability to build a relationship with that person is enhanced.

Questions related to future needs will help your team recognize opportunities to pursue, once any remedial problems are addressed. These questions might include the following:

- *What are the most important goals or initiatives going on in your company right now?*

- *What trends are impacting the way you do business, or expect to do business, in the future?*

- *How is your job changing? What do you find most challenging?*

- *How are your customers' requirements changing?*

- *How is _____ likely to affect you (e.g., technology, globalization, the recent merger, growth, decline, changes in the economy, changes in regulatory requirements, etc.)?*

Action

After team members have conducted their discovery interviews, the next step is to plan the appropriate actions. This is an activity that works best with the entire team present because there will likely be actions that can be done once on behalf of the entire customer organization, versus having several team members duplicate efforts. What also sometimes happens is that different customers request different approaches. Perhaps some like the quarterly face-to-face meetings with your team, and others feel twice a year would be sufficient.

As you and the team members explore the feedback you received, you'll find that there are three levels of response that should be considered:

1. Individual-level responses are focused on one person's feedback and do not impact others. Examples include:

   Provide new contact with a copy of the briefing document we prepared on our company.

   Explain how and when enhancements to electronic ordering will be implemented.

2. Team-level responses impact many or all of the individuals with whom your team interacts, and they should become part of the team's response to the customer. Examples include:

   Explain the new product rollout schedule, including marketing support and anticipated pricing.

   Present results of research conducted on end-users.

3. Organization-level responses are required for issues that are systemic in nature and beyond the scope of the account team to resolve. Examples include:

   Create a bill that will consolidate the four sets of invoices currently received.

   Enhance the technical specifications document to include cross-references to old part numbers.

"Organization-level issues" are one of the reasons we have written IMPACT *Without Authority*. Although some of these issues are beyond the scope of you and your account team's ability to resolve, we want you to find ways to influence the organization on any issues that are creating barriers to growth in your account.

> **This is exactly why functional employees – either your account team members or other non-team employees – need to conduct discovery interviews—so that you are not the only one who hears the customer's pain around the issue.**

For example, it will be much easier for you if the IT person goes back to the programming team and recounts the stories related to the confusion of invoices. As a peer, the programming team will also find it more believable.

As a team, you also need to be thinking in terms of current versus

"Our customer kept telling its account manager that it wished the invoices would be printed 'landscape' instead of 'portrait' to be consistent with its other paperwork. Thinking this was just not something he was going to put ahead of everything else on his mind and the other major projects he had for IT, his response was that it couldn't be done. It turns out that it was an easy change, but this was only discovered when IT got directly involved in the discussions."

future. The team needs to ask itself:

- *Which actions are related to our current performance and need to be resolved before we can grow the relationship?*

- *Then, once the "remedial" issues are addressed: What are the opportunities for us to grow this relationship?*

Experience

The critical third step is ensuring the customer experiences the actions you implement. What do we mean by that? Most importantly, communicating your plans to the customer, and then continuing to provide status updates. The customer won't always experience what you've done if you don't communicate. Remember, the customer is quite busy, and won't necessarily notice your implementation of change.

Best Practice

"A large agricultural products company was instituting discovery interviews throughout the division, and one salesperson strongly resisted having a manufacturing person involved. 'These are my relationships to manage,' she said. She was eventually required to take the plant scheduler with her to the buyer, and in that particular session the buyer explained the impact on his business when they couldn't make last-minute weight changes to how their order was packed. This was an issue the salesperson had discussed before with the plant, with the scheduler insisting they needed 24-hour notice for changes. However, after the interview, the customer had a new advocate on site—the scheduler himself. 'Our customer needs to change the palettes tonight; this is important!' he is now often heard to say. What was the difference? Hearing the voice of the customer directly."

The experiences you create for employees involved with these activities will help you as you navigate your way internally.

Your Executive Sponsor

There are many reasons to have some kind of executive sponsorship program. The involvement of your company's executives can augment your efforts to gain higher access in your customer's organization. When your customer's executives know that you have executive support and quick access to resources, they are more likely to involve their executives in the relationship.

Another function of executive sponsorship is to help you break down some of the barriers you are facing. As executives become more involved with your account, they will also become one of your strongest customer advocates. Just as you found yourself advocating more strongly for your customer the more you got to know them, so will your sponsor. By helping your executive sponsors form relationships with their peers in your customer organization, you will be developing another internal ally.

Perhaps you have an executive sponsor assigned to your customer, and your company has well-established guidelines for that role. Even if that is so, executives need very specific direction regarding with whom they should be dealing and what their role should be. When you first meet with your executive sponsor, explore how you can utilize him most effectively. Questions you should ask you sponsor include:

> "There's share of wallet and then there's share of mind. The sponsor's role is not to manage the account. It is to win the mind of the client. The account team will manage the wallet."

- *Have you been an executive sponsor before? What worked? What didn't?*

- *What would you like to know about this customer?*

- *How would you like to spend your time with this customer?*

- *What kinds of information do you want to receive from me on an ongoing basis?*

In addition, relate the following kinds of information to your sponsor:

- Historical sales;

- Any issues in the relationship;

- Who the decision-makers and key influencers are;

- How buying decisions get made;

- How you feel the sponsor could contribute to success with this account; and

- Your vision for the future of this account.

Consider how one SAM from a multi-national corporation gained full advantage of his company's executive sponsorship program.

The corporation implemented a program called Senior Executive Relationships (SER) as a management engagement process to entwine its executives with major customers. As part of the SER methodology, over 250 senior executives call on the company's 35 largest key accounts. Since the program's implementation, business from these accounts has grown 5%—while the rest declined.

If you are fortunate enough to have a program like SER that formalizes senior-level support for your strategic account program, the process that follows will help you keep and expand that participation. If senior-level support is insufficient or lacking, communicating the following process is imperative to demonstrating the need to establish one of the most critical components of a successful strategic account management program.

Best Practice

A global account manager (GAM) relates the following details about how he utilizes the SER program. We think he is a master at creating IMPACT without authority!

"One of the requirements of SER is that each GAM must have at least eight contacts with our company's top executives. I have 15! I take advantage of the formalized structure of the SER program to execute management contacts and to achieve alignment from top to bottom within my global account. I probably have relationships with 100 people within my company, not to mention another 100 at my customer's.

I think an executive interface is essential. I truly believe in the power of peer-to-peer meetings where my CEO meets with my customer's CEO. I know my customer's CEO and can meet with him alone, but a biannual peer-to-peer meeting is important to establish and strengthen a significant partnership relationship between our two companies. I do not attend these meetings, but I coordinate them and brief my CEO on three or four (never more) subjects to discuss. I use a high-level customer contact to find out what is on their CEO's mind before the meeting, and after the meeting things trickle down to various groups in each organization that I pursue one-on-one.

I also conduct two or three senior executive calls a month of my own. After the meetings, I arrange multi-day planning sessions to review key strategies with the senior executive and his management team that interfaces with my customer around the globe. I call these meetings 'Customer Day' and I find that customers love to tell their major suppliers where they are going and what they need to get there. In the evening I arrange a social activity and sit my people next to their customer counterparts so they can form relationships. I use Customer Day to initiate and action plan; 90 days later I respond to the executives to let them know what has been accomplished."

Executive Assistants as Allies

Discussions about executives should include at least a few words about the executive assistant (EA). One of your primary allies in the effort to gain visibility and support from senior management is the executive assistants that report to them. You know how important your relationship with various gatekeepers at your customer's company is. Your relationship with the EA of your CEO or senior leadership team is just as important in keeping SAM on the radar screen of your own company. How can you gain his or her support for your cause?

No one makes a more effective coach than the assistant to the CEO or other top level executive. They know exactly what is going on. They can separate essential information from "white noise." They can move your report to the top of the pile or pack it for airplane reading, schedule a meeting at the best time of day or follow up frequently to obtain the information you need. As you build your internal network, don't forget this key person!

> "There are certain things that a CEO, CFO or executive vice president can do, like open doors or resolve conflict, that an account manager just cannot do. The executive / client interface gives a strong differential advantage over the competition."

Other Senior Executives

If your company does not have plans to establish executive sponsors, think about how a senior executive could still be beneficial to your customer and to you. The absence of a formal program does not prevent you from seeking the help of a senior executive in your account. When you ask for his or her involvement, be specific about the contribution you believe could be made to the success of your account, as well as why the customer would appreciate the relationship. You will be most successful if you try to engage an executive who has genuine interest in interfacing with a customer; the worst that can happen is they say "no thanks" and you try again with someone else. Then, simply follow the guidelines we outlined above for establishing a relationship with the executive and for defining your respective roles.

Customer Satisfaction Surveys

Many companies obtain "voice of the customer" feedback from customers through telephone or mail surveys. Surveys are often seen as a means of making the customer's voice heard in the organization, but there are a few problems that can get in the way of this happening effectively.

First, the various functional organizations might be accustomed to being shown only problems. For example, someone (you?) goes to them with a comment such as, *"We took a hit last quarter in our customer satisfaction tracking, in the question 'Orders are complete and on time.' Can you tell me what was different, and what we are doing now?"* When only the problem areas are highlighted, the surveys become associated with negative feedback.

Another potential problem is that the feedback is not customer-specific. Perhaps special processes have been established for the strategic accounts, but their responses are most likely getting buried in all of the other customers' responses. To treat a strategic account as an anonymous customer, whose voice is blended in with all other customers, is a contradiction that minimizes their importance. You should not call an account strategic only to turn around and ask for their feedback in a non-personal, low-effort manner.

Yet another problem could be that the customer survey is not obtaining "actionable" feedback, and without additional information, the functions truly are not sure what to do next. One mistake that many organizations make when they design a survey is to design mostly quantitative questions. For example, *"On a scale from 1-to-5, how would you rate our product quality?"* Although scores provide directional and trending information, telling you *what* to focus on, they typically offer very little in the way of *how* to improve. In addition, over time the quantitative scores tend to reach a plateau from which improvement is difficult to detect or achieve.

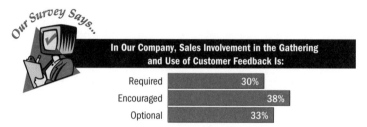

In Our Company, Sales Involvement in the Gathering and Use of Customer Feedback Is:	
Required	30%
Encouraged	38%
Optional	33%

Source: 2001, Survey on Leading-Edge Practices for Measuring & Managing Customer Loyalty, SAMA, PDI, IMPAX.

Here are some tips for enhancing the usefulness of customer surveys:

- Be vocal about you, as a SAM, having your information needs considered when the survey is designed. Don't simply be silent recipients of data.

- Be sure the survey includes open-ended questions. Regardless of how you are obtaining feedback (i.e., telephone, mail, Internet), several open-ended questions should be included asking for suggestions as to how your company's products or services should be improved, as well as what the customer likes most about them.

- In telephone and Internet surveys, any low score on a quantitative question should prompt a follow-up question asking the customer to explain his or her answer.

- The survey should also ask for positive comments; these open the door to hearing compliments that can be passed on to the appropriate employees. We've walked through call centers in which signs hanging above employees' cubicles include customer

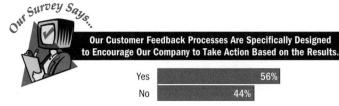

Our Customer Feedback Processes Are Specifically Designed to Encourage Our Company to Take Action Based on the Results.

Yes   56%
No   44%

Source: 2001, Survey on Leading-Edge Practices for Measuring & Managing Customer Loyalty, SAMA, PDI, IMPAX.

quotes of exceptional service. All the quotes were obtained directly from the customer satisfaction surveys that asked for what the customer found most positive.

Summary

Although creating a "customer-centric culture" is usually thought of as a top-down initiative, this chapter pointed out many things that you, as a SAM, can do to foster such a culture from your vantage point.

Answer the following questions to focus your next steps:

1. How have I been successful in creating internal customer advocates in the past?

2. Who else seems to be successfully creating customer advocates for their account? What are they doing, or how can I find out?

3. What could I be doing more of now?

4. What should I encourage my peer group of SAMs to do that would increase the level of customer advocacy in our company?

Chapter 6:
Determine Organizational Feasibility

We hope you are beginning this chapter with a solid network across various functions and geographies (see also Chapter 4). However, we realize that you may have picked up this book because you need to influence now and don't really have time to build new internal relationships. That's OK, although recognize that it might be a little harder to obtain some of the information you need. As we mentioned when we explained the "stairs", you don't have to climb one at a time; it's just easier that way.

Think about the following scenario: You have a great idea. It's something your customer needs, and you're convinced it will lead to increased sales and customer loyalty. Your passion is hard to contain, and if passion were all it took to get organizational buy-in, you'd be there.

But of course, passion is not enough. In fact, passion in the absence of organizational benefit could make it harder for you to influence others in the future (remember credibility back in Chapter 3). This chapter will help you be objective and thorough in your analysis of what it will take for your company to implement your idea.

We'll start again with a self-test. As with other chapters, use your low scores as a guide to those areas on which you'll want to place more emphasis.

"What makes a good SAM? The ability to create immediate understanding as to the importance of what we're trying to do for the customer, yet make it immediately relevant to even the smallest entity of the team or the organization."

	Strongly Disagree	Somewhat Agree	Strongly Agree
	1 ------- 2 ------- 3 ------- 4 ------- 5		
1. I understand how to convey to others the driving reasons for my idea.	1 ------- 2 ------- 3 ------- 4 ------- 5		
2. In addition to articulating my idea to others, I include a detailed set of business-as-usual assumptions.	1 ------- 2 ------- 3 ------- 4 ------- 5		
3. I understand how to determine the effects of my idea on different parts of the organization.	1 ------- 2 ------- 3 ------- 4 ------- 5		
4. I know how to identify the broad range of people and functions that I will need to influence in order for my idea to be implemented.	1 ------- 2 ------- 3 ------- 4 ------- 5		
5. I work to identify all the effects that my recommendation might have on my company.	1 ------- 2 ------- 3 ------- 4 ------- 5		

From Concept to a Detailed Plan

This chapter will walk you through the steps needed to move your idea from a concept to a plan. Detailed steps for determining the parts of your company that will be affected by your idea are provided.

As you go through the three steps below, notice that your demeanor, which is dictated by how you want to be perceived, will change from step to step:

	Objective of this step	How do you want to be perceived?
I. Define the need for change and the base case.	Convey the driving reason(s) for your idea to your company.	Factual. Non-judgmental.
II. Present your initial idea.	Obtain resources to help you further study your idea.	Enthusiastic. Humble. Seeking approval.
III. Develop the Implementation Plan.	Cover all the facts. Find sponsorship and allies within your company.	Open. Seeking understanding. Empathetic, yet challenging.

I. Define the Need for Change and the Base Case

Your starting point for new ideas is to articulate the reason(s) you began to think of the idea.

Think of your idea in terms of proposing change. Many of the concepts of change management are relevant if you think of your idea in this context, one of the most important concepts being that others are less apt to resist change when they fully understand and embrace the reasons for it.

Be explicit about the reasons you are asking the organization to consider your idea. There could be either internal or external factors that are driving your idea, although more often you'll find it's an external customer-driven cause that you are representing. Use the following as a guide to articulating the driving factors behind your idea:

Driving Factors	
Internal Factors	**External Factors**
· Is there an opportunity to leverage an already-developed product, service or technology into something new for your account?	· Has your customer identified an opportunity that would increase your business with it?
	· Is your customer complaining about some aspect of your product or service?
· Have efficiencies been developed inside your company that could benefit your customer?	· Is your customer concerned about something internal to its business with which you could help?
· Are current trends, such as in the areas of labor, material costs or other products / services, a threat to your product or service's future viability?	· Has your customer expressed needs that you are not able to meet with your current product / service mix?
	· Are competitors moving in a direction that threatens to leave your company behind?
	· What might happen if the idea you have is not implemented? For example, is it more likely that a competitor could steal customer share from you? Or that your products or services will become obsolete?
	· Are external trends, such as regulation, technology or drivers of demand, a threat to your product or service's future viability?

Inherent in defining the drivers behind your recommendation is defining its potential value to your company. As you work to define the value your solution will bring, consider the questions below, which suggest a number of benefits that might result from your idea.

In Barbara Geraghty's *Visionary Selling©*, the following 20 questions are suggested to demonstrate the value of your solution. You won't find that all 20 are relevant for every idea that you propose, but you are likely to find several that will bolster your idea's standing.

Ask yourself, "How will my solution":
- Increase sales?
- Enable us to raise prices?
- Enable us to sell more in existing markets?
- Enable us to expand into new markets?
- Increase profits without requiring more capital?
- Decrease returns?
- Decrease COGS (cost of goods sold)?
- Decrease SG&A (sales, general & administrative) expenses such as headcount, offices, research and marketing?
- Increase efficiency?
- Drive costs out of the supply chain?
- Increase cash?
- Decrease inventory?
- Decrease receivables?
- Decrease taxes?
- Decrease debt?
- Help us manage assets more wisely?
- Enable us to generate more revenue from assets?
- Increase shareholder equity?
- Enable us to revitalize or divest of a losing operation?
- Allow us to divest land / buildings or machinery / equipment?

In addition, think how your solution might:
- Increase customer loyalty;
- Result in a stronger market position for your company;
- Address competitive threats;
- Increase capacity to serve the customer; and
- Support the achievement of corporate strategic initiatives such as globalization.

Consider the following questions for creating linkages with your own corporation's goals:

1. *What is my company's corporate strategy; i.e., what businesses do we want to be in?*

   • This is important, because the greater the fit between your ideas and your company's strategies, the easier it will be to get immediate attention. By keeping your company's strategies in mind, you will also be more likely to look for opportunities that are a good fit when you are with your customer.

2. *Which businesses are considered 'core'? Which are not?*

- Again, when you are proposing something that will contribute to the success of your company's core business, you will find it easier to get visibility and to gain acceptance of your ideas.

3. *What are my company's most important priorities?*

- If conserving cash is a priority, significant outlays for new capital will be hard to justify.

Once you've defined the reasons you're recommending change, define the base case, or business-as-usual scenario. The purpose of your base case is to paint a picture as vividly as possible regarding the current state of doing business. Extrapolate business-as-usual over a period of time long enough to compare to the eventual business case you develop. Define as accurate and believable a scenario as possible, from current sales to organizational implications.

As you define the business-as-usual scenario, create a clear picture by incorporating both internal and external assumptions. Consider the following questions as thought-starters.

Business-as-Usual Assumptions	
Internal Assumptions	**External Assumptions**
· What are your current sales projections?	· From which other suppliers does your customer buy related products / services?
· What is the product / service mix your customer currently buys from you?	· What is your "share of customer"?
· What are the relevant costs to serving this account?	· How loyal is your customer?
· What divisions sell into your account?	· Who are your most significant competitors?
· What geographies sell into your account?	
· What does it take for your organization to serve this customer now?	

Be specific about the assumptions you are making because variations in these assumptions will eventually be incorporated into your scenario testing. As you develop an implementation plan, you might find that there are other assumptions that need to be included in your base case, as well.

II. Present Your Initial Idea.

When you first start presenting your idea to others, your objective should be to simply gain their support for studying the idea.

Initially, you are not asking for buy-in to the idea; you are asking for buy-in to consideration of the idea.

There is a big difference. Although you will convey a certain level of enthusiasm, you also want to be clear that you don't yet know whether it is a viable idea, which is why you need the participation of your peers—so that you can determine if this will be both a win for the customer and a win for your company.

Use the following as your agenda for this meeting.

Agenda
· Introduce your idea.
· Why is your idea needed?
· What is the current base case?
· Why should your company consider this idea?
· Gain agreement to investigate further.

- **Introduce your idea.** Briefly introduce your idea and your reason for meeting, which is to gain support for further investigating the feasibility of your idea.

- **Why is your idea needed?** Clearly define why you think this idea should be considered. The *driving factors* you outlined in Step I should be openly stated with as much substantiation as possible.

- **What is the current base case?** Use the *business-as-usual* assumptions you've outlined. Again, include as much substantiation as possible, including historical data to support the realistic view you are providing. Because your goal is to gain support to spend time investigating the feasibility of your idea, the more information you can provide that your audience will embrace, the more successful you are likely to be.

- **Why should your company consider this idea?** Explain how your idea supports the achievement of corporate or divisional goals, priorities or strategies. Include an overview of the benefits that you believe could be realized. This could be as simple as "I believe this idea will generate $300,000 in new sales." Or it might encompass a broader set of organizational goals such as, "This could help us establish our first Latin American servicing operation, which in turn would enhance our market share in that region of the world."

- **Gain agreement to investigate further.** Be as specific as possible about who you would like to be involved. If you can, provide an estimate of how much time will be needed to complete this investigation. If you need resources that will cost money (e.g., market research and development of prototypes), be open about that need.

> *A successful outcome of this meeting, or more likely this series of meetings, is the agreement that time will be spent investigating the feasibility of the idea.*

III. Determine Impacts.

Once you've obtained buy-in to the investigation of your idea, the next step is translating your vision into a tactical plan. Your objective during this stage is to fully understand the potential effects of the idea that you are proposing. This requires you to be open to others' ideas and comments. Although you might feel that their reactions are unnecessarily negative or challenging, it is actually to your benefit to hear such comments now. Listening openly to skepticism, and then working with others toward a solution, will better position you for seeking final approvals.

Since this is when the proverbial rubber meets the road in terms of influencing others, it is critical that you:

> *Involve others as you develop your plan. One of the mistakes we see from SAMs (and others who are trying to influence within their organization) is that they work independently until the last step when they present their idea to the final decision-makers.*

Any plan will be more accurate if you've included people who know the subject. People are also more apt to support ideas they have contributed to developing, so you can save yourself time and effort by including them early. In addition, the senior management of the affected functions or regions will be more inclined to support something they know their own people support and have been involved in.

The more complex your idea, the more likely it is that you will need a "formal" project team. If you're lucky, you already lead a cross-functional account team. In this case, after asking for its involvement (don't assume that just because they are part of your account team, you shouldn't follow all the steps outlined previously), you will call on your account team members as needed.

If you do not have a formal account team, an alternative is to create a special project team for your idea. This alone might be difficult; if your company has not acknowledged that resources should be made

> "To really have a strategic relationship with a global customer, you have to get buy-in at all levels. First of all, you have got to get buy-in at the uppermost level—for instance, the president of both companies who can support the initiative and say 'Here's the message from on high.' And that's good—you have to have that. But the key really is that layer of management in the middle. Senior management can go forth and get together and do a lot of things and make a lot of promises. But it's middle management – and I'm talking about a director-level, business manager-level – that level is the one that really has to have the buy-in because they are the ones that are going to do all the work or shut everything off."
>
> *Director Strategic Accounts, U.S. based Fortune 500 Chemical Company*

available for an account team, then finding resources to create an implementation plan might not be possible. If this is the case, the time you have spent establishing an internal network will pay off. People will be quicker to return your calls and help you develop the information you need to build a plan.

If your idea, and the resultant implementation plan, is not complex, a "virtual" team (which is not a team in the true sense of the word but is more accurately described as a group of people you simply call) might work.

Your Target Audience

We refer to your target audience as "who" you will need to influence to get your idea approved. Not surprisingly, the more complex your idea, the larger the number of people needed to support your proposal.

We see most ideas that SAMs propose fall into one of the following categories. Each will be addressed separately.

Category 1: Changes to Current Products or Services
Category 2: Introduction of New Products or Services
Category 3: Changes in Distribution by Business Units or
                Geographies
Category 4: Pricing Changes
Category 5: Organizational Changes
Category 6: Partnership / Alliance Opportunities

Category 1: Changes to Current Products or Services

To fully understand what it will take to implement your idea, create a visual map of how you currently do business with your account—i.e., what are the inputs, and how do they get transformed into the outputs you deliver to your customer? Start with a macro view, and develop increasing levels of detail as you drill deeper into the various steps. One approach to accomplishing this is by way of seven-step process flows.

What we mean by seven-step process flows is this: you can define what just about any organization does for its customer in seven steps or less. We can describe an entire corporation in six! Here's a manufacturer of appliances:

A Ficticious Company

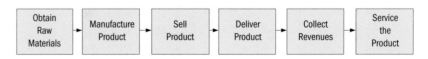

Circle each step that will be impacted, even in a small way, by your idea. Too simple? Of course, but it's only meant to be a starting point. You can now take any one of those steps, and define up to seven sub-steps. Perhaps the "service the product" step is one that will be most impacted by your idea. Its seven steps might be:

Again, circle the step(s) that will be impacted. You might create another level of sub-process flows, or you more likely will simply document beneath each step where the impacts will be felt. Understanding the detailed steps within the larger processes is important in order to accurately assess, and develop an appreciation for, the impact that your idea will have on the organization. Alternatives might also become evident more quickly.

This can be a valuable group exercise. People like to share with others what their organization does and how. Each person who shares such information will feel appreciated, and the other participants will also learn more about your business. The end result can be used to define the array of individuals or functions you need to influence.

Category 2: Introduction to New Products or Services

You can follow a similar approach with a new product or service idea. Speaking with your product development personnel is generally the right first step to take. From there, the team can develop the seven-step process flow charts. It will probably take your team longer than identifying the impact of changing a process, especially if this is a product or service quite different from any you currently supply.

Category 3: Changes in Distribution by Business Units or Geographies

Developing process flows works best, of course, when you are looking at your business from a process perspective—i.e., how things get done. A different level of complexity is introduced when there are multiple geographies or multiple business units that already are, or could be, selling to your customer. If this is the case, you need to examine, in a different way, where the impacts of your idea will be felt.

To start, develop a table in which you identify every entity, including business units and geographies, and their involvement with your customer. The purpose of this exercise is to identify the various impacts that your idea might have. In the following table, you might identify the five columns as the business units of "Office Products", "Network Products", and the countries "France," "U.S." and "Canada." In this example, although there is overlap between the sales made by the Office Products division and Canada, they are both entities within your company that are held accountable for results. Therefore, they should be unique columns. You might need more copies of this table.

Once your column headings are defined, simply check off each cell that is relevant. Perhaps Canada reports revenues to the account and services them, but does not manufacture product nor view your account as a key.

Example

Entities

Involvement With Customer	Office Products	Network Products	France	U.S.	Canada
Reports revenues to my account.	√	√	√	√	√
Has employees who sell to my account.	√	√	√	√	√
Considers my account "key".	√			√	
Services my account.	√	√	√	√	√
Produces product for my account.	√	√	√		
Conducts R&D.	√	√	√		

Entities

Involvement With Customer					
Reports revenues to my account.					
Has employees who sell to my account.					
Considers my account "key".					
Services my account.					
Produces product for my account.					
Conducts R&D.					

The entities defined in the top row of the table will be put into the Influence Map on page 114.

Category 4: Pricing Changes

There seems to be no end to the pricing challenges customers present. Whether it is their own uncertain economic climate, the competitive industry in which they operate or a procurement director that is pushing for price relief, you will likely be faced with asking your own organization for pricing decisions at some point in time. And your requests might not always be for lower prices; you might actually believe there is an opportunity for increased pricing.

Your requests for pricing changes are supported by rationale that positions your company either on the defense or the offense.

- One offensive position emerges when you can explain that price relief to the customer is accompanied by some kind of opportunity. The opportunity is usually significantly increased sales, but might also be the use of the customer's resources or access to its intellectual capital.

- You are also playing offense when you propose price increases. Perhaps you believe your price does not accurately reflect the value of your product / service, or you feel that the market will bear a higher price and the increased margins can be wisely utilized.

- If you are on the defense, it is usually because you believe you will lose significant amounts of business unless you are able to implement the reduction in price. Your competitors might be making aggressive moves in the marketplace, or perhaps your customer is threatening to shift share to a competitor.

If price decreases are viewed as a singular event, there will never be financial justification for them. It is up to you to be sure this is not how price decreases are viewed. If you believe that *not* lowering price will cause a significant loss of business, include that analysis in your proposal. Similarly, proposals to increase price, if viewed in isolation, are likely to be met with skepticism.

It is critical that you obtain external facts in order to justify your request for a pricing change. This might include intelligence regarding competitive products and services, customer data that documents market trends or customer discussions that include the entire horizon of why price decreases are requested.

Similar to defining the entities that will be impacted by changes in "who sells what", determine the entities that will be impacted by potential pricing changes by answering the question:

> Which entities report revenues for the products / services that will be impacted by this pricing change?
> -
> -
> -
> -
> -
> -
> -
> -

Transfer the names of these entities to the top row of the Influence Map on page 114.

Category 5: Organizational Changes

Most often it is a vice president of sales – not the SAM – who advocates for organizational change. More specifically, the organizational change that readers of this book are most apt to propose is how a company's strategic accounts should be managed. Anyone who has ever launched a SAM program knows that there are many stakeholders who have a keen interest in understanding how the proposed strategic accounts program will impact them.

Nonetheless, this is a less likely scenario for you, the reader of this book, and the book's purpose is not to guide you through the details of how to re-structure your organization. We'll simply suggest a similar framework for identifying who you will need to influence.

	Entities				
Involvement With Customer					
Reports revenues for any of the strategic accounts.					
Has employees who manage any of the strategic accounts.					
Services the strategic accounts.					

Category 6: Partnership / Alliance Opportunities

One last category in which we've seen SAMs strive to create influence is in recommending a partnership. Partnerships can range from informal or verbal agreements to legally defined ventures. The investment of time required to make the partnership successful increases with the more there is at stake. Therefore, the justification for a complex agreement needs to be better defined and solidified.

To identify who you will need to influence, begin by defining the processes, products and / or services that the partnership will impact. The tools outlined in the previous five categories are useful in your analyses here as well. For example:

- If you are proposing to outsource certain services, which parts of your company will be impacted? The process flow analysis on page 108 will help.

- If you want to partner with a company that offers complementary products or services, who sells the corresponding products / services in your company? Use the grid on page 110. Instead of asking which entities "sell to your account," ask yourself which entities would be affected by sales of this product / service.

The goal is exactly the same as it has been thus far—determine who will be affected by your recommendation so you can investigate the feasibility of your idea.

The Influence Map

Once you have identified *who* in your organization your idea is likely to impact, you can begin to define *how* they will be impacted, what changes are required and what they will cost.

Use the target audience defined in your process flows and matrix diagrams to populate the top row of the following chart. Since each entity in your targeted audience will become a unique column on this chart, you will probably need to make multiple copies of it. The chart will help you understand what it will take to obtain buy-in to your idea. As development of your tactical plan evolves, you typically discover more people who should either be directly involved in creating the plan, or from whom you need input.

Keep in mind the following guidelines as you complete the Influence Map:

- The map is conceptual. You will find that its little squares are much too small for some complex parts of your business, yet they might be overkill in some other areas. Summarizing information in the document is often a useful approach.

- You might feel that there is too much detail required for some small changes. It's OK to skip over some of the cells; again, use the template as a guide. Think through everything carefully, however, as you do not want to later find yourself in a meeting with a decision-maker who brings up a factor that surprises you.

Remember, being over-prepared is much better than being under-prepared!

Influence Map				
1. Function / Organization that will be impacted by my solution:				
2. What kinds of changes will they need to make?				
3. Who needs to approve the changes that will be needed?				
4. a) What is the *best case* estimated cost of these changes?	Fixed: Variable:	Fixed: Variable:	Fixed: Variable:	Fixed: Variable:
b) What is the *most likely* estimated cost of these changes?	Fixed: Variable:	Fixed: Variable:	Fixed: Variable:	Fixed: Variable:
c) What is the *worst case* estimated cost of these changes?	Fixed: Variable:	Fixed: Variable:	Fixed: Variable:	Fixed: Variable:
5. On a scale from 1 (resistant) to 5 (agreeable), how receptive will they likely be?				
6. If less than agreeable, what will his / her greatest concern(s) likely be?				
7. Do I have a relationship with this person? If not, who can I work through to get to him / her?				
8. How can I use the customer to help me influence?				
9. Why should this person agree to my proposal?				

Answer the questions listed for each function or entity that will be affected if your solution is implemented. For those functions that will be affected in multiple ways (e.g., both process changes and investments required), you might want to use a separate column for each source of change that requires a different decision-maker.

Use the following guidelines as you complete the chart.

1. *Function / organization that will be impacted by my solution*: On pages 108-113 you identified various entities (i.e., functions, business units, geographies) that will be impacted by your proposal. Enter them in this first row. Test yourself by ensuring you've answered any of the following questions that are relevant:

   - Who will create the product or service I am proposing?
   - How will the product / service be delivered?
   - Who will service it?
   - How will it be invoiced?
   - How will returns be handled?
   - What existing products or services will be impacted by this proposal?
   - Whose revenue results will be impacted?
   - Whose costs will be impacted?
   - Are there any labor issues?
   - Is capital investment needed?

2. *What kinds of changes will they need to make?* The kinds of changes required might include:

   - Changes to existing processes; i.e., changing the way they currently do things. Document the details of the changes required, such as "intervene to collect all invoices and consolidate into one bill" or "route calls from customer to special team."
   - Implementing new processes.
   - Systems / technology changes.
   - Product enhancements or changes in specifications.
   - Service changes.
   - Allocating resources to an initiative.
   - Training.
   - Distribution.
   - Results achievement (e.g., budget overruns, sales underruns).

3. *Who needs to approve the changes – including any effects on measurements – that are needed?* Think in terms of the following guidelines:

- If an organization's ability to achieve any of their key results is going to be affected, the most senior executive of that organization will need to be involved. That executive may not be willing (or able) to make the change without approval from his boss, who is likely the president of the division or the CEO of the corporation. Do not expect that you will be able to accomplish what you want without the proper levels of decision-makers involved! See Chapter 8 for more on how to approach this scenario.

- Any impacts on expense lines will need to be approved by the budget holder. Even though one person might have responsibility for operations in a certain area, he or she may not be the budget holder for expenditures needed such as training, equipment, software, personnel or materials.

- Recognize that any proposed change to how employees accomplish their responsibilities has the potential for meeting resistance. You might find that the decision-maker will face strong opposition from others in the organization who have more direct influence than you do. They will take the opportunity to make a case for why your assumptions are faulty.

4. As you better understand how your idea will impact each function or entity, you will not always know exactly what the costs will be. The people you are working with can give you a good understanding of the "what if" scenarios to build. For example, perhaps it is not known whether employees will need eight or sixteen hours of additional training. This variability must be built in, so that in your "best case" scenario the costs of training are eight hours per person, in your "most likely" scenario perhaps twelve hours would be reflected, and in your "worst case" the full sixteen hours would be incorporated.

To fully account for costs, think broadly. Consider both fixed and variable costs:

Fixed

- Training and other personnel needs, such as hiring.

- Product / service development and engineering costs.

- IT and systems development costs.

- Marketing costs.

Variable

- Sales of other products or services that might be affected by your idea.

- Cost of materials.

- Production / packaging / delivery costs.

- Invoicing costs.

- Selling costs.

You might also be able to offset some of the costs with savings—e.g., productivity improvements, materials, business development. Document these as well.

Worst-case scenarios should also incorporate any risks to successful implementation. For example, what if you can't get the IT system changes in the timeframe required? What are the chances of that happening? What would be the consequences of a delay? As you work with your network to build the plan, include the following questions in your discussions:

- *What are the risks facing this implementation plan?*

- *What is the probability of each source of risk?*

- *What is the degree to which it will affect the final outcome, or will it affect any other parts of the plan?*

- *Do any of these risks need immediate attention?*

- *Do we need a plan to manage the risks?*

- *What is the cost of contingency plans, should the risks be realized?*

5. On a scale from 1 to 5, where 1 = Resistant and 5 = Agreeable, rate how receptive you think the decision-maker in this function is likely to be.

6. If your answer to Question #5 was not a "5", document why you do not expect them to agree with your idea. Consider the following impacts that might concern them:

   - Ability to achieve any of their key results;

   - Headcount;

   - Other expense lines such as hardware, software, equipment, training, hiring, supplies, travel and facilities;

   - Capital investments;

   - Resources (including staff) required to plan the initiative; and

   - Loss of focus on other areas critical to them.

7. *Do I have a relationship with this person? If not, who can I work through?*

   - Ideally, you already have a relationship with the person. If you have been laying a foundation properly, you will be able to approach them, confident that you know how you will be perceived.

   - A formal account team helps you make connections with the decision-makers you need. Determine who on your team can help you reach the people you need.

   - If you do not have an account team member who can help you, consider the other relationships in your internal network.

8. *How can I use the customer to help me influence?* Your internal network might be skeptical of the solution you are proposing. They might feel that the customer is not committed to the changes you're recommending, that your company won't achieve the levels of success you are suggesting or that it simply isn't worth the effort required to implement your idea.

   - Consider how you might utilize your customer to help your cause. This could include having the customer write a letter endorsing your idea (or expressing its dissatisfaction with the current state), or asking them to meet with some key individuals in your organization about the idea.

- Consider including a customer representative as part of your solution development team. They can address first-hand any issues related to them.

9. *Why should this person agree to my idea?*

- You will be more assured of agreement if your idea will directly benefit that person's organization or function within the organization. Sometimes an acceptable payback period is required for the investment of resources, so you will need to demonstrate that. And of course, the shorter the payback period, the better.

- Less compelling, but also helpful, is whether your idea will benefit that person in some indirect or intangible way. Will he or she be better positioned in your company? Will your idea open the door to other opportunities he or she wants?

- The most difficult scenario is when your idea benefits the overall corporation, but does not benefit, or even hurts, this organization. This often happens in multi-national corporations, where one country or region sacrifices revenues or margins because of a global agreement. The case study in **Chapter 10**, our **Message to the CEO**, opens with an example. On a smaller scale, it could simply be that your customer service organization is asked to increase headcount expense to support the belief that decreases in share of customer will result if they don't.

Your conclusions to these questions will guide you in determining how you present your ideas in the remainder of this chapter and the following two chapters.

Developing your Influence Map is key to understanding what it will take to get your idea approved. The map becomes your guide to documenting the cost of implementation and the names of the people from whom you will need to gain approval.

Summary

You may have viewed this chapter as a bit overwhelming and containing too much detail to be practical. When we first described the "stairs" to the impact model, we mentioned that climbing stairs becomes automatic—that you won't really need to think about it as you do it.

With that thought in mind, we encourage you to use this chapter as a reference, if not as a guide (i.e., you might find that you want to look up certain ideas as needed, rather than conducting your analysis step-by-step as described). Whatever means you use to make the thought processes become automatic will be to your ultimate benefit, because the decision-makers in your company whom you need to influence will be asking the questions that this chapter prepares you to address.

Answer the following in order to create your action plan:

1. As I analyze ideas that have been rejected, the following are the ways I did not properly prepare:

2. I should become more disciplined about the following steps (check any that apply):
__ Define the base case and need for change.
__ Present the initial idea.
__ Develop an implementation plan.

3. I would like to improve my own skills in the following areas:

Chapter 7:
Apply Influence Skills

David B. Peterson, Ph.D.

The past few chapters have focused on better understanding the organization in order to build the support you need for your idea or solution. Along the way, however, you inevitably deal with an "individual," not an "organization." You just identified a number of those individuals in your Influence Map in Chapter 6. Building a compelling and logical business case is necessary – but not sufficient – for success. The skills required for influencing others are addressed in this chapter.

Think about what it means for you to influence someone. Most people describe influence as "getting someone to do what I want them to do." Now put yourself in the other person's shoes—how does it feel when someone tries to get you to do what they want? Like most people, you are probably put off by that, which is exactly why that approach rarely works. In fact, taking that approach leads some people to use manipulative techniques that create resentment and make future interactions more difficult.

> **A more effective approach is to view influence**
> **as a search for a win-win solution.**

This search is not just a facade for getting people to do what you want, but is a means for gaining genuine commitment to a goal that serves both of you. Finding the real win-win ensures that you get what you are looking for, simultaneously building trust and a better working relationship, so that future conversations become quicker and easier.

As you take the following self-test, think about how these questions support a win-win result. Keep the results in mind as you read the rest of this chapter.

	Strongly Disagree 1 - - - - - 2 - - - - - 3 - - - - - 4 - - - - - 5		Somewhat Agree		Strongly Agree
1. Before trying to influence people, I make sure I understand what is important to them (i.e., their goals, values and concerns).	1 - - - - - 2 - - - - - 3 - - - - - 4 - - - - - 5				
2. I am genuinely curious about other people's opinions on important topics.	1 - - - - - 2 - - - - - 3 - - - - - 4 - - - - - 5				
3. I check out underlying assumptions before proposing a course of action.	1 - - - - - 2 - - - - - 3 - - - - - 4 - - - - - 5				
4. I consistently search for solutions that meet the needs of all parties.	1 - - - - - 2 - - - - - 3 - - - - - 4 - - - - - 5				
5. I almost never have to go back and get people to follow through on their commitments to me.	1 - - - - - 2 - - - - - 3 - - - - - 4 - - - - - 5				
6. I remain flexible in influence situations so I can find a solution that everyone supports.	1 - - - - - 2 - - - - - 3 - - - - - 4 - - - - - 5				
7. When the conversation is not going the way I desire, I probe to gain a deeper understanding of the other person's concerns.	1 - - - - - 2 - - - - - 3 - - - - - 4 - - - - - 5				

Getting to the Heart of Influence

What derails most influence attempts is that people jump to a solution too quickly. They come up with a recommendation that meets their own needs, but without adequate consideration of the needs and concerns of others.

Like most SAMs, you are in your position because you're a good problem-solver. You scope out a customer situation, find an astute resolution to the problem or opportunity and then try to gain others' buy-in. Yet, even when your solution is brilliant, they push back. Why? And what can you do about it? The answer is found in the following three basic principles of win-win influencing.

Clarify what you want. Pick a situation – something big – in which you need to influence someone right now. What do you want from them? More than likely, you've already phrased your need in the form of a solution. It's like someone standing in front of a hotel saying, "I need a taxi." What you really need is transportation to the airport—and by focusing on one preset solution, a taxi, you rule out other possible solutions, such as a hotel van, airport shuttle, a friendly stranger heading to the same destination or perhaps the subway or train. Much better to ask, "What's the best way to get to the airport?" (Depending on your priorities, you could also ask for the quickest, cheapest or easiest way.) By focusing on the underlying need, you remain open to a wider range of solutions. It even frees you up to brainstorm more creative possibilities: What about a helicopter?

Thus, you begin the influence process by utilizing one of your selling (to customers) skills with yourself—i.e., determine the underlying needs. By clearly stating your needs, you are essentially identifying your own criteria for a good solution:

- Gets me to the airport;

- At least one hour before my flight leaves; and

- Price comparable to a taxi ride or less.

Go back to the situation that you face and consider three questions:

- *What is the preferred solution that you've already identified?*

- *What are the underlying needs that you wish to address? Examine what you like best about your own solution and what you don't like about other possible solutions. Both perspectives will point you toward important needs. Keep in mind that some of your needs will be business objectives, and some will reflect personal values and priorities, such as the desire to look good, make more money, get visibility, make a difference or feel valued. Be honest with yourself about what really motivates you in each situation.*

- *What other options do you have for meeting those needs? Although this moves toward solving the problem, it's a useful exercise to determine if you've surfaced all of the relevant needs: As you articulate why you don't like various alternatives, you identify additional criteria for a successful solution. Generating a list of options helps you stay flexible and avoid premature closure.*

The first few times you answer these questions for important influence situations, write down your list of needs to help you articulate exactly what you are looking for. This helps you focus and explain your criteria clearly to others.

Discover what matters to others. There are two reasons for taking the time to understand others' perspectives. First, you can't design a solution unless you know what you're dealing with—you simply have to understand the playing field if you want to succeed. Second, expressing an interest in others builds the rapport and trust that you need for effective working relationships. The time you invest now reduces friction and saves valuable time later.

To understand someone's agenda, ask them questions such as the following:

- *What is your goal? What are you trying to accomplish?*
- *What are the key issues from your perspective?*
- *What concerns do you have as we try to solve this?*
- *What criteria should we use to define the best solution?*
- *Personally, what are you hoping for in this situation?*

If they've given it any thought, the people you are talking to may already have jumped to their own solution. If that happens, ask them:

- *What problems does that solve for you?*
- *What do you like about that approach?*
- *What do you see as the main limitations of other potential solutions?*

> **To fully understand another person's agenda, you must temporarily set aside your own agenda to influence.**

You even have to let go of your drive to solve the problem. Your only agenda at this time is to understand this person's needs and how he or she views the situation. Only when you have that information can you proceed.

As simple as it sounds, you need to practice this skill diligently, or your ingrained habit of driving for a solution will prevail and you will find yourself quickly becoming impatient with the process. Trust us—if you don't take the time to discover what matters now, it will invariably cause greater delay and frustration downstream.

The other challenge in discovering what matters to others is that you will only learn half the story. Although they will be comfortable being candid about the business issues, they will be relatively quiet on the personal and political impact unless you have established a high level of trust. Understanding this latter aspect is essential, because that is where most attempts to influence fail completely: Even when your business case is sound, people may be reluctant to support it when they stand to lose something they value. In fact, if you've ever asked yourself in frustration and amazement, "How can they not support this?" you have been caught in this trap.

The following ideas will help you dig beneath the surface to discover what motivates their behavior.

Ask tactful yet direct questions.

· What is the personal impact if we proceed on this?

· What is the worst that could happen to you in this?

If you listen without judging, they may share one or two sensitive issues. Always assume there is more that they are not saying. Remain silent and wait for an answer to show your interest is sincere.

Offer tentative hypotheses.

· I imagine that if we go that route, your team will take some heat.

· When we've done this in the past, it hasn't always reflected well on the person who has to make the call. Let's see what we can do to avoid any collateral damage to your area.

· If I were in your shoes, I know I'd be concerned about what's going to happen to me.

By floating some potential issues and showing your interest in their well-being, you make it safer for them to acknowledge their concerns and perhaps offer more.

Observe them carefully and reflect on their reactions.

Because you always have to assume that there is more than they are saying, watch carefully to see what type of ideas they support or reject. Consider what they stand to lose or to gain. People are only human, after all, and they care about such things. Each person is different, though, so consider a broad list of goals and values that each person might care about: money, position, power, prestige, security, reputation or legacy, close friends or colleagues who might be affected, opportunities to learn something or try something new, having an impact, a sense of personal control and autonomy, time and resources, life balance, etc.

Remember, influencing is not only about logic, it's about what matters to people.

The people you deal with already have a rational argument to support their point of view. You have to combine the business logic *and* the personal logic to get the best outcome. Once you know what someone cares about, you can start to design solutions that address their concerns and provide enough of what they care about so they can support you. For example, allowing a person who values visibility to join you in making a presentation to the board can facilitate his or her support of your proposal.

Find a solution that addresses both your needs and their needs. Here's where the influencing process gets easy, because most people are good problem solvers *once the underlying needs are clearly defined.* After you have done your homework and have a complete list of the relevant criteria, you can put those problem-solving abilities to work. Generate ideas that might work, and test them against the criteria. If a solution meets all the criteria, use it. If it doesn't, set it aside and continue brainstorming. If it comes close, you might want to play around with it later and see if you can find a way to make it work.

The secret is to be firm on needs and flexible on solutions.

If you have a long list of criteria, or if some of them seem in conflict (e.g., maintain consistency in the product line, and at the same time customize to a specific customer request), you may have to explore more creative options. It takes a few minutes for people to let go of their assumptions and really take a fresh look at the problem in front of them, so allow some time for creativity and great ideas to emerge.

The key to success is to be just as committed to ensuring that their needs are met as you are to ensuring that your own needs are met.

Now that you're familiar with the major elements of influence, let's look at a step-by-step process for your conversations with people. Each of the above fundamentals is embedded into a key part of this process.

The LETS Influence Process

LETS stands for Listening, Exploring, Talking and Solving. The acronym is helpful as a reminder that getting to the solution is essential, as is talking to present your case. However, listening and exploring come first. The LETS Influence process has eight steps, as presented on the next page.

The process begins with two simple steps that usually take less than a minute:

1. **Make a personal connection.** For someone you know well, this may be as simple as saying hello. For people you don't know well, greeting them, thanking them for the opportunity to meet and asking about their day will often suffice. Cultural differences may dictate what is involved here; for example, some Asian cultures have a formal and lengthy process for building the relationship and establishing roles before any business topic may even be broached.

2. **Frame the conversation** by setting clear expectations for what you will talk about, what outcome you seek and how you would like to structure the conversation. A comment as simple as, "Have you got a minute?" quickly communicates that you have

LETS Influence Process: Listen, Explore, Talk, Solve

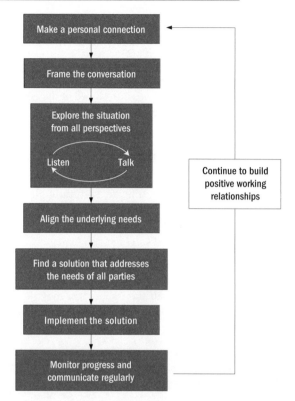

a brief and easily resolved topic that can be handled informally. Similarly, a written meeting agenda listing topics and times serves to frame a more formal and structured conversation.

Be honest about your intentions. Sometimes people say, "I'd like to understand your views on XYZ Corp." when their real purpose is to try to gain support for their own position. You will get more respect and more cooperation if you say, "I'd like to make sure we understand what's happening at XYZ Corp. from each of our perspectives, and then plan a course of action that we can both support."

The more difficult or emotional the topic, and the more conflict or disagreement that you expect, the more you need to frame the process you will use to structure the conversation. Referring back to the three main influencing elements outlined earlier in this chapter, you might say, "I'd like to start by telling you how I see the situation, then make sure that I completely understand your perspective. Then, let's look at our options to see if we can find a win-win solution. Finally, if we have time, we can start planning our action steps."

Next comes the heart of the influencing process, where you will spend most of your time and where you will find the real leverage for aligned solutions.

3. **Explore the situation from all perspectives.** Two of the three key influencing principles that we introduced at the beginning of the chapter belong in this step:

   - Clarify what you need; and

   - Discover what matters to others.

   As noted above, even when you understand the objective business needs, take the time to sort through the personal, political and subjective landscape from all perspectives, including your own. The next table shows some of the distinctions between exploring (step three) and solving (step five).

Because it has been repeatedly reinforced that we should find solutions quickly, we aren't even aware that we have jumped to a solution before examining all the issues. You may need to remind yourself to adequately explore the situation from all perspectives before proceeding.

Are You Exploring or Solving?	
Exploring	**Solving**
Exploring refers to the process of understanding the nature, scope and underlying cause of a problem or situation, including other people's needs and concerns.	*Solving is the process of identifying potential ways to resolve a situation, deciding on and planning a course of action.*
· Attempting to understand the nature and scope of the problem.	· Finding potential answers to the problem.
· Figuring out what really matters to people, including yourself.	· Making decisions about what to do next.
· Suspending your judgement until the picture is clear.	· Choosing a course of action.
· Searching for the root cause.	· Searching for the best options to accomplish the task you've identified.
· Checking underlying assumptions.	· Proposing action steps.
· Trying to understand the real needs of all stakeholders.	· Searching for a solution that addresses the needs of all stakeholders.
· Clarifying the requirements for a mutually acceptable solution.	· Evaluating how well different recommendations meet the specified requirements.

The following may signal that you are jumping to a solution too quickly. Shift back to exploring when you:

- Enter into negotiations with your final position already in mind instead of suspending your conclusion until a range of options is considered;

- Try to convince others to do it your way rather than subjecting all possible solutions to an objective analysis;

- Treat the other person as the opposition rather than as an ally in finding a win-win solution;

- Argue over who is right rather than working together to find a mutually agreeable solution;

- Look for the weak link in others' arguments rather than trying to generate creative solutions that everyone can support;

- Become frustrated when others keep repeating themselves, instead of probing to understand why they feel they need to repeat their message; or

- Find yourself repeating your own message, instead of exploring both sides to facilitate a common understanding of the situation.

In addition to balancing the complementary tasks of exploring and solving, you need to manage both talking and listening. Although the distinction seems elementary, it's not uncommon for people to use questions to promote their own point of view while appearing to be listening. Therefore, be aware of your own intentions: Are you truly trying to understand them or are you trying to get them to see your point of view?

> "Internal selling is not about closing a deal, it's about communicating."
>
> *Michelle Lapierre,*
> *Director, Sales Integration & Development,*
> *Global Sales, Marriott International*

Are You Listening or Talking?	
Listening	**Talking**
Listening involves drawing out others so you fully understand their perspective (i.e., thoughts, goals, needs, values, concerns and feelings).	*Talking refers to presenting your perspective (i.e., thoughts, goals, needs, values, concerns and feelings) so that others understand where you are coming from.*
· Working to understand others' ideas, views, goals and feelings.	· Presenting your ideas, views, goals, or feelings.
· Summarizing their position.	· Explaining your position.
· Trying to understand the other person's view and rationale.	· Selling your view and rationale.
· Showing that you understand all their main points.	· Making sure you are thoroughly understoood.
· Reading their body language and nonverbals.	· Using nonverbals that show your reactions to what others are saying (e.g., nodding your head, rolling your eyes).
· Asking questions that encourage people to say more about what is really on their minds.	· Asking leading questions.
· Demonstrating curiousity about other people's views.	· Asking questions when you already know the answer.

In the exploring phase of influencing, you present your own views as well as listen to others. It's easier if you do this as two separate and distinct parts of the conversation, rather than blending them together. When you listen, explore their views thoroughly. When you talk, lay out your perspective clearly and completely. Sometimes this doesn't work as well as you'd like, so here are a few tips (at the end of this chapter you'll find additional advice on listening):

• Be clear and deliberate on what you are doing and where you are in the conversation: Are you talking or listening? Are you exploring or solving?

• Decide who talks first and who listens. If you initiated the conversation, present your message first. Explain the purpose of the conversation and describe your needs, goals, thoughts and concerns. Keep your opening message succinct. Give the headlines now and fill in the details later. If they initiated the conversation, keep listening until you fully understand their needs.

• Shift to listening as soon as possible, as soon as the other person understands your major points. If they interrupt, explain that (based on your framing of the conversation from step 1) you are very interested in understanding their point of view after you lay out your own thoughts. Of course you want them to interrupt to ask clarifying questions, but defer any debate until later. If they interrupt you several times or they appear to be getting frustrated, shift to listening. When attempting to influence someone, it is far better to err on the side of listening. Set aside your views and go wholeheartedly to exploring their point of view. Don't go back to talking unless they specifically request it or they have finished talking.

- Once you understand their message, shift back to talking and fill in the details on your message as needed. Do not let yourself get into a debate over any one point. Generate a list of issues from each perspective but don't worry about resolving anything yet.

> *The goal of exploring is not to get agreement,*
> *but to gain mutual understanding.*

- Shift back to listening at any point in the process when:
  - They appear to resist your message;
  - You find yourself in a power struggle;
  - You don't understand why you aren't making progress;
  - Either one of you keeps repeating the same message. If they repeat themselves, write their point down and make a comment along these lines: "OK, that's an important point here. What else are you concerned about?" If they repeat the point again, refer to the written note and say, "I've made a note of that. Is there something that I'm missing? Otherwise, I'm interested in hearing what else you have to say";
  - Either of you is becoming frustrated or angry; or
  - You don't know what else to do.

- When you think you have heard their full story, summarize the needs that have been identified and ask if there are any more.

A useful technique for exploring is to actually write down, on a flipchart or whiteboard so that everyone can see, the criteria for each person or perspective. A common situation for SAMs might look like this:

	Customer	Sales	Production	SAM
Objective Needs	Reduce costs.	Meet quota through this sale.	Maintain margins and consistency in pricing structure across customers.	Grow total revenues for the account.
	Greater customization to meet needs.		Reduce cost structure.	Increase cross-selling.
	Quicker response time.		Adapt to increasing expectations for speed and customization.	Change the sales culture.
	...All of the above, toward the greater goal of remaining competitive.			Elevate the customer's view of the company.

Some of these needs are potentially in conflict—reducing costs for the customer and increasing sales for you appear, on the surface, to be in opposition. However, a win-win can be established if, for example, a long-term relationship is established that generates ongoing revenue, or if the savings from cost reductions can be split among the parties. These solutions generate value for both parties.

A second potential conflict emerges when unspoken personal needs are considered. A salesperson who values money highly – even one who recognizes the need to reduce internal cost structures – may push for a deal that generates high revenue and high commissions over a deal that is more efficient and less costly to provide to the customer. Similarly, a production manager who values power and being in control may subtly drag his or her feet in response to constant requests to meet customer needs. Again, even when they themselves may see flexibility and meeting customer needs as important, their desire to maintain power and control is a critical component in shaping the outcome. If you want the production manager's full support for your idea, you need to provide a sense of power and control for them in some way. Similarly, your own needs – for example, to increase your visibility and impact in order to advance your career – shape the nature of the solution that you will find acceptable.

Finally, most of the needs listed in the table, such as reducing costs (which shows up for both the key account and for production) are actually still solutions. By repeatedly asking, "What problem does that solve?" you move closer toward understanding the real needs. A key account that is demanding lower costs is often struggling to remain competitive or remain profitable. Once you have surfaced all the concerns, you shift the conversation to questions such as, "How can we work together to help you remain profitable?" This approach builds a stronger relationship and gets closer to solving the root cause issues both of you face.

4. **Align the underlying needs.** After you have identified everyone's needs and concerns, put them together into one list that defines a single problem that you must solve collectively. Reinforce the shift by pointedly rewriting all the criteria onto one list. Emphasize that now you are all working together on the same issue. This has two significant benefits. First, it puts all of you together on the same side of the problem. Instead of opponents trying to influence each other, you are now teammates trying to work things out for everyone's benefit. This shift in perspective often generates a dramatic change in people's attitudes about working together. Second, by focusing on the complexity of the real issues, you are capable of finding a solution that truly resolves the situation. Everyone will be committed to making it succeed because it meets their needs.

5. **Find a solution that addresses the needs of all parties.** By focusing everyone on a common problem with one set of criteria, you harness everyone's natural desire to problem-solve. The problem is now more complex because more variables are involved. You may need to spend a few minutes helping everyone step back from their assumptions, so encourage creativity and brainstorming. If someone is not happy with a solution that looks good, it almost always means that an important criterion has not been surfaced. Shift back to exploring and work patiently to surface the need. It may feel like you are stepping back and even wasting time, but it is a common and natural part of the process. Once you identify a solution that meets all your criteria, ensure that a concrete action plan is put together. Have everyone review the plan to ensure that it still meets their needs.

6. **Implement the solution.** As important and challenging as the implementation step is, there are no special insights here relative to the influencing process, so we shall move on to the next step.

7. **Monitor progress and communicate regularly** to provide ongoing accountability and surface any issues promptly. Follow-up is essential to ensure that people don't get distracted by other crises or priorities. By periodically touching base with people and reviewing progress, you remind them of their commitment and may identify problems early so that they are relatively easy to resolve. Schedule brief but regular checkpoints and be sure to hold yourself accountable for making sure they happen. Even when they seem trivial, they are an important element in completing any major task. Making sure that everyone delivers on their commitments and / or remains updated on status is an essential part of the influencing process. Following through also builds your credibility.

8. **Continue to build positive working relationships.** In today's ever-changing world, you never know who you will be dealing with again. Take advantage of the trust and momentum you've built by staying in touch with people over time. Keep them as a part of your network so that the next time you need to influence, you start with a strong foundation.

More Tools for Influencing

In the remainder of the chapter, we offer some additional tools that can boost your success in influencing others.

Strategic Listening

You have probably been exposed to listening skills classes more than once in your career. Here's a quick snapshot of an approach called strategic listening, which emphasizes a focused search for precisely the information you need to understand to accomplish your goals. It's not merely actively listening to what a person says, but a way to structure and guide the listening process so you don't waste time listening to people talk about unrelated topics. Strategic listening requires that you be clear on what you are trying to understand. For example, if you are trying to influence a customer to give you more business, you need to understand at a minimum how they view you and your competitors, what they are looking for, what they are afraid of, what matters to them personally and what other expectations and pressures they are experiencing from those around them. Once you are clear on exactly what you need to understand, start using these five components:

Open Attitude. Enter the conversation with a sense of curiosity and openness to whatever is said. Set your own agenda aside and focus solely on understanding people's perspectives. Whether you agree or not is irrelevant. In fact, you should avoid saying, "I agree" or "Yes, that's right" – even as a way to build rapport – because it can set up a sense of evaluation and judgment. People may feed you what they think you want to hear, or they may assume that if you remain silent on some point you disagree. Better to just listen and explore.

Open Questions. Ask straightforward questions to explore others' point of view on the topics in which you're interested. Ask the same question in different ways to show your interest and help them look at the topic from multiple angles. For example: "What do you value most in a strategic partner?"; "What is essential to you in a strategic partnership?"; "What aspects of partner relationships have been most valuable and most difficult to you so far?" As they talk, you can ask more specific follow-up questions to zero in on critical issues, such as: "How do you see the impact of technology on partner relationships?" Avoid leading questions that are really just a projection of your own position, such as "If we use the right technology, don't you think that strategic partners can be located anywhere?" Leading questions are talking, not listening, and will fail to explore the other person's beliefs.

Identify Emotions. As people talk, listen for their feelings. Simply naming the emotions the other person is conveying (e.g., "Sounds like you were really frustrated"; "So you felt pleased with the new direction"), demonstrates that you understand and makes them feel more at ease in opening up to you. When in doubt about a negative emotion they are feeling, try using one of the two most encompassing emotion words: concerned and frustrated. Even something as simple as "You sound frustrated" conveys a deeper level of understanding and interest.

Nonverbals. Everyone knows how important nonverbals – eye contact, facial expression, posture, vocal tone and inflection, etc. – are for conveying a sense of interest and engagement. We'll simply add the idea that there are two goals of listening. First, make sure that you understand the other person's point of view. Second, make sure they feel like they've been heard. Even when you are truly listening, if you don't *act* like you are listening, people may conclude you're not really interested and you damage the trust that you are building.

Silence / What Else? One of the most useful questions in the world is "What else?" Use this two to three times after every open ended question to convey sincere interest and get them to think through their answers at a deeper level. Almost everyone is prepared to give a safe and straightforward answer to your questions. When you ask, "What else?" and then wait silently for them to answer, you allow deeper reflection to occur. The most valuable answers almost always come later in the conversation, once you've moved through the surface level responses. Allowing them time to think fosters trust, communicates your interest in what they have to say and allows them to discover deeper insights.

Silence makes many people uncomfortable. You will be tempted to fill the silence by asking another question or sharing some other idea. Resist. Use the discomfort generated by silence to encourage them to fill the void by sharing more of their perspective.

Finally, a note on what lies at the heart of communication between people: The best open questions in the world – or any other technique, no matter how skillfully used – will never facilitate communication as effectively as genuine interest and an open attitude. Even with the clumsiest skills, if you are sincerely interested in what the other person has to say, they will open up to you. On the other hand, if you are impatient and eager to accomplish your personal agenda, your attitude will diminish even the smoothest techniques.

The Big TOE: Theory of Everything

The title of this tool is offered slightly in jest, but it actually contains more than a grain of truth.

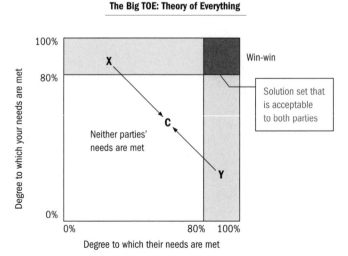

The Big TOE: Theory of Everything

This diagram illustrates why many attempts to negotiate, influence, solve problems and even lead organizations can end up in failure. Start with the y-axis, which depicts your needs. Imagine X is your solution to a problem. You are satisfied with this, because it meets the majority of your needs. The party with which you are dealing is not happy with your proposal, however, because it doesn't even meet half its needs as depicted along the x-axis. In contrast, it is proposing solution Y, which obviously is inadequate from your point of view.

This is the most common situation when two parties meet: each one has a proposal that works great for them but not for the other. Typically, they then start negotiating tradeoffs between X and Y, so they each move closer to the mid-point. Eventually, they agree on a compromise solution C. However, neither is satisfied with the outcome, because it doesn't meet anyone's needs at any reasonable level. To make matters worse, both resent each other because they each gave up a lot and don't feel the other side appreciates what was done for them!

This is why so many apparent agreements end in failure. No one is committed to implementing the agreed-upon solution, because it doesn't really work for them. So both parties walk away disgruntled and searching for other ways to get their needs met. A month later, when no progress is evident, each party has a convenient excuse in terms of how other things have come up that have just kept them too busy to fulfill their commitment on this. In a Dilbert fashion, both sides may expend some effort in order to look like they're fulfilling the agreement, but they never put their heart into it.

The answer, as described in the first half of the chapter, is to set your preferred solutions aside and keep in mind the three key principles of win-win influencing:

• Clarify what you want;

• Discover what matters to others; and

• Find a solution that addresses both your needs and their needs.

As you can see, the space for a solution that satisfies both your needs and their needs is smaller than a solution that just meets your needs. So you may have to be more creative. Obviously, this works to the advantage of both parties. The unanticipated value of this approach is that creative solutions often lead to new insights, new business opportunities and even newer sources of competitive advantage. It's a way to explore solutions that have never been tried before and see where they lead you.

Pro and Con Analysis

When you find yourself in a debate between two solutions, and you can't seem to shift the focus to exploring needs, pro and con analysis is a tool that may help. It's another way to shift from resisting your opponent to putting both of you on the same side in searching for the best solution for everyone's needs.

In most situations where people are advocating their views, one person will point out all the advantages of his or her view (Solution A) and all the disadvantages of the other (Solution B; and so on through Solution C and D or however many proposals there are). The advocate of Solution B is only talking about the advantages of his or her position and the disadvantages of all other solutions. In effect, everyone is avoiding the discussion of the flaws of their own solution and the merits of other people's proposals. As a result, they debate but never engage in a true dialog with each other that might result in a deeper understanding for both.

	Positives	Negatives
Solution A	• • •	• • •
Solution B	• • •	• • •
Solution C, and so on	• • •	• • •
New or modified solution, based on exploring all the needs	• • •	• • •

Copyright © 2002, Personnel Decisions International Corporation. All Rights Reserved.

A pro and con analysis removes the conflict from a discussion by getting everyone working on the same task with the same purpose. It involves an objective and systematic review of the advantages and disadvantages of all solutions.

It works through the simple creation of a diagram such as the one above. The only task is to accurately and objectively list the positives and negatives of each proposal. The obvious way to begin is simply by asking for the positive aspects for Solution A, then the negatives for Solution A. Everyone should participate in this equally. Those who support Solution A, as well as those who oppose it, should be able to identify positives as well as negatives. Then you move on to the other proposals. Almost always, getting people to focus on developing an objective analysis improves cooperation and communication, and it may even lead to a breakthrough in resolving the conflict.

If you are the proponent of Solution A, the best way to launch this activity is by talking about the areas that you are not naturally inclined to discuss (i.e., the negatives of your own proposal and the advantages of Solution B). By doing so, you demonstrate your objectivity and your commitment to finding the optimal solution. Other people will feel pressure to appear more objective as well. You can then draw them out and encourage their objectivity by asking them to list positives and negatives for each solution.

As people talk about the positives and negatives for various proposals, comments rooted in their various needs and concerns will start to surface. This often allows you the opportunity to shift gradually to a more exploratory discussion of those needs and concerns. At some point, you can suggest that a joint search for a new solution – one that meets everyone's needs – might be beneficial.

What If You Still Don't Make Progress?

Despite your best efforts, you may still find yourself in a situation where you aren't making sufficient progress. Consider whether the following are getting in your way:

They don't trust you. There are many reasons why people may not trust you—your past relationship with them, their relationships with other people in your role, they don't know you or they just have a hard time trusting anyone. One of the ways to build trust is to share more of your needs with them. By taking the first step in disclosing your own motivations, you may be able to get them to reciprocate. If that doesn't work, remember that influence grows over time. In the future, focus on building relationships with key people before you need them. Identify the people who are most critical to your success and find ways to foster a better working relationship over the next few months so you have some traction the next time you seek to influence them.

You're still pushing your own agenda. If you pretend to listen and explore other people's ideas, but in reality act like you are just searching for ways to pitch your views, people will retrench in their own positions. You have to really let go of your solution and focus on meeting everyone's needs. Focus on your primary goal—finding a solution that works for everyone. Be willing to compromise. Know which battles to fight.

You've raced too quickly down the path. Sometimes you may feel like you've done everything right, and then you hit a barrier where you can't make further progress. This almost always indicates that one of two things has occurred:

- You haven't identified all the important needs they have. Listen better and pay more attention; or

- You came up with a solution that doesn't really meet everyone's needs. Either you're still pressing your own solution too hard or you aren't placing enough importance on their needs.

You might have to back up and work through the process again, building on the work you've already done. Influence is a cyclical process. Remind yourself that taking the time now spares you time and aggravation in the future.

If you try all of these suggestions but are still at an impasse, several options remain.

- Ask the person you're trying to influence for help. Point out that you've been trying to find a win-win but it doesn't seem to be working. Ask them what it will take to make progress. Invite them to work with you to figure out a way to move forward.

- Find a place to start. See if you can find a small step on which you both agree and use it as a pilot to generate some momentum.

- Get help from someone else. Find a neutral person to facilitate your conversation.

- Escalate the discussion and involve higher management. Chapter 8 will address this in more detail.

Summary

We hope it is evident by now that influencing works best when you are committed to finding a solution that benefits everyone. You may have to let go of your pet proposal, but in the long run, you will only benefit more. Even if some of these recommendations seem challenging, we encourage you to experiment with them. Try them out where the risks are moderate and see what happens. What surprises most people who use the LETS Influence process is that spending time listening and exploring actually makes their work more efficient because it:

- Addresses the root cause(s);

- Identifies and deals with important concerns and barriers; and

- Finds a solution that people are committed to, so the topic doesn't need to be revisited.

Complete the following action plan for yourself.

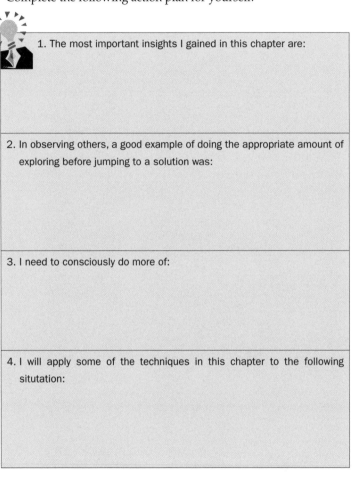

1. The most important insights I gained in this chapter are:

2. In observing others, a good example of doing the appropriate amount of exploring before jumping to a solution was:

3. I need to consciously do more of:

4. I will apply some of the techniques in this chapter to the following situtation:

Chapter 8:
Involve Senior Management

The previous five chapters were focused on helping you achieve IMPACT without authority through a "bottom up" approach (i.e., you navigate the organization, build relationships, analyze all aspects of your solution and develop solid rationale for your recommendation). You will now be interfacing with senior management in your company because they are often the decision-makers whose buy-in you need for your ideas. This chapter will provide you with tools for interfacing effectively with them.

In an ideal world, all the work you've done thus far, and will do as you complete financial analyses, will get you the approvals you need. However, you don't live in an ideal world, and sometimes escalation to higher-level executives is needed. We have already drawn attention to various scenarios in which you need to employ this as a top-down strategy to influence others.

If escalation is required, it does not mean that all the time spent approaching the problem from the bottom-up is wasted. Most senior executives will ask you the kinds of questions that you can only answer if you've implemented the steps already described.

"There's always wrestling for resources and the difference for the global account is you've got teams that, because they work inside of their accounts, are much better at assessing the market place, understanding the real size of the opportunity and then presenting that opportunity to the resource managers inside of our firm. So, it's a much more professional approach to serving customers instead of tin-cupping for help with the account—it's a formal, explicit process supported by real business case information. I've been in national accounts teams and everybody is screaming for resources but they don't have @$*&! for a business case."

Take the following self-test to help frame your thinking as you read this chapter:

	Strongly Disagree 1 - - - - - - 2 - - - - - 3 - - - - - 4 - - - - - 5	Somewhat Agree	Strongly Agree
1. I understand when it's important to involve senior management in the influence process.	1 - - - - - - 2 - - - - - - 3 - - - - - - 4 - - - - - - 5		
2. I know what is important to senior management, so that I can make my ideas compelling to them.	1 - - - - - - 2 - - - - - - 3 - - - - - - 4 - - - - - - 5		
3. Senior management understands the complexities that our strategic account managers are trying to navigate.	1 - - - - - - 2 - - - - - - 3 - - - - - - 4 - - - - - - 5		
4. I understand the financial metrics that are important to senior management, and I use them to demonstrate the impact of various decisions.	1 - - - - - - 2 - - - - - - 3 - - - - - - 4 - - - - - - 5		
5. I know how to test the financial viability of my recommendations.	1 - - - - - - 2 - - - - - - 3 - - - - - - 4 - - - - - - 5		
6. I am able to accomplish basic levels of change / customization for my customer fairly easily.	1 - - - - - - 2 - - - - - - 3 - - - - - - 4 - - - - - - 5		
7. I know how to develop the components of a compelling presentation when I seek final approval for my recommendation.	1 - - - - - - 2 - - - - - - 3 - - - - - - 4 - - - - - - 5		

Preparing to "Think Like an Executive"

In Chapter 6 we walked through the three key steps needed to move your idea from a concept to a plan. This chapter focuses on the continuation of that process—conducting the appropriate analyses to justify your decisions and get the approvals you need. In addition to these steps, this chapter covers the use of escalation as a strategy.

	Objective of this step	How do you want to be perceived?
I. Define the need for change and the base case.	Convey the driving reason(s) for your idea to your company.	Factual Non-judgmental
II. Present your initial idea.	Obtain resources to help you further study your idea.	Enthusiastic Humble Seeking approval
III. Develop the implementation plan.	Cover all the facts. Find sponsorship and allies within your company.	Open Seeking understanding Empathetic, yet challenging
IV. Analyze the financials.	Create an accurate financial assessment.	Analytical Objective As having a desire to be thorough
V. Make a business assessment.	Assess your idea as an outsider would (and will).	As balancing passion for your company and passion for your idea
VI. Present to decision-makers.	Assuming it is a good idea, gain approval.	Passionate Factual Thorough

For some of your recommendations, the tools presented in previous chapters might be enough. If your recommendation affects only one or a few entities, the exploring and discussions you've had could very well be sufficient to get the approvals you need. This will not always be the case.

Regardless of the complexity of your recommendation, you should be comfortable with the ideas in this chapter. Although complex ideas take longer to analyze, simpler ideas should be able to stand up to the same kind of thought process. The rationale for them is just easier to complete and understand.

IV. Analyze the Financials

You may or may not need to build a financial business case to support your recommendation. As we mentioned, many times simply presenting compelling rationale will get you the approvals you need. However, if your idea is a complex one, or one that crosses the silo walls of multiple entities, you may need to develop the financial justification.

How does your company make financial decisions? If cash flow is the most important consideration in decisions, you will need to demonstrate how your idea impacts it over time. If EVA (economic value added) is the primary determinant of new initiatives, you must understand that it is required, and know how to calculate it.

If there is not an established method for preparing a financial analysis for new initiatives, be prepared to demonstrate:

- The degree to which sales and margins will outweigh costs;

- The payback period for any investments to be made;

- The level in the organization at which the business case is most compelling—and the level(s) that are less likely to see the benefits;

- How your proposed idea supports key goals of your organization; and

- Any leverage you might gain from this solution.

There are entire textbooks written on financial measurements and how they are used in decision-making. We are not attempting to replace those resources with this chapter. If you have attended even a basic course on "Finance for the Business Executive" you are not likely to need these next few pages. However, if you are a novice in this area and you want to get your feet wet – or you can gain approval for one of your ideas by using some basic financial metrics – then this may be just what you need.

Choose the Right Analytical Tools

Two of the simplest and most frequently used financial analysis techniques are the *cost / volume / profit analysis* (also known as *break-even analysis*) and the *payback method*. These techniques, discussed more specifically on pages 147-149, are relatively simple and will be adequate in many situations. Keep in mind, however, that *cost / volume / profit analysis* and *payback method* are only two tools out of the many your organization may use to evaluate proposed investments. Before making a major investment proposal, it is wise to discover which investment analysis methods are accepted in your organization for proposals such as yours. Find out how proposals similar to yours were pitched successfully in the past, and learn from them.

If the proposed investment requires a major capital investment (new equipment, for example) or the benefits will accrue over multiple years, decision-makers may require a more sophisticated *discounted cash flow* analysis that takes into account the time value of money. Ask someone in your finance function to assist you.

When there are multiple entities involved, be they business units or geographies, your financial analysis must take into account the sum total of all financial impacts.

However, remember that any one decision-maker will be interested primarily in the impact on his or her own organization and financial commitments.

Many a SAM has run into the problem of creating a valuable solution at the corporate level, only to have it undermined by individuals in a business unit or a country that would be impacted negatively.

Break-Even, or Cost / Volume / Profit Analysis

This is frequently the best analytical tool to use for new product introduction or pricing decisions. For a cost / volume / profit (CVP) analysis, you need to know the relationships between fixed and variable costs, selling price and unit sales. For new product decisions, a CVP analysis will help you determine the sales volume needed to recover your costs. A CVP analysis can also help you determine the increase in sales volume needed to justify a price decrease.

Example 1: New Product Introduction

Fixed costs: $250,000
Variable costs: $3500 per unit
Selling price: $4000 per unit

Number of units that must be sold to break even
= Fixed Costs ÷ (Unit Selling Price − Unit Variable Costs)
= 250,000 ÷ (4000 − 3500)
= 500

Conclusion: If you sell more than 500 units of the new product, it will generate a profit. Below 500 units, the new product will lose money.

Challenge yourself:

• *How realistic is it that you will sell 500 units? What has your company's experience been with rolling out new offerings like this in the past?*

• *Will any other products experience a decline? If so, how many additional units might need to be sold to offset the loss of those sales?*

Example 2: Price Decrease

Current selling price = $400
Variable cost per unit = $200
Expected unit sales at current selling price = 1,000
Proposed price reduction = $40

If you reduce the price by $40, you will reduce profits by:
(Unit price reduction × unit sales)
= $40 × 1,000 = $40,000

To make up for this, you need to sell more units. But how many more?

Incremental unit volume =

(Price reduction × Current unit sales) ÷ (Proposed price − unit cost)

$$= (\$40 \times 1000) \div (\$360 - \$200)$$
$$= \$40{,}000 \div \$160$$
$$= 250 \text{ units}$$

To help others understand your analysis, it would be helpful to present a side-by-side comparison of the current situation and your proposed price reduction:

	Current	Proposed	Difference	% Difference
Price per unit	$400	$360	-$40	-10%
Unit volume	1000	1250*	+250	+25%
Sales revenue	$400,000	$400,000	--	--
Variable costs per unit	$200	$200	--	--
Profit per unit	$200	$160	-$40	-20%
Total profit	$200,000	$200,000	--	--

Break-even volume

Once you have done the calculations, you should assess the likelihood that the $40, or 10%, price reduction will actually result in a 25% increase in sales. Anything less than a 25% unit volume increase will decrease profits; anything greater will increase profits. If you believe the 25% increase is achievable, you should seek out supporting evidence to make your proposal.

Offsetting price decreases with volume increases will be hardest to achieve on your lowest margin projects or services. In this example, if variable costs had been higher than $200, the increase in unit volume to break even would have been greater than 25%.

Payback-Period Analysis

The payback period is the expected length of time it will take for the returns on the investment to equal the initial cash outflow. It is best used for short-term projects of less than a year since it does not take into account the "time value of money" (i.e., a dollar received today is more valuable than a dollar received in the future, because the dollar received today can be invested).

Many organizations commonly use the payback period to assess proposed investments. All other things equal, decision-makers will consider an investment with a shorter payback period to be a safer investment. The payback period method is most useful when the costs and benefits can be predicted fairly reliably. When your cost / benefit figures must be estimated, use conservative estimates to make your analysis more credible to decision-makers.

Company Y sells widgets for $100 per unit, with a profit margin of $40 per unit. The company sells 10,000 widgets per month. The company is considering changing its raw materials supplier because it will save $1 per unit. The changeover would require an initial investment of $12,000.

Initial investment: $12,000
Monthly savings = Savings per unit × Units sold per month
          = $1 per widget × 1,000 widgets sold per month
          = $1,000

Payback period =
Initial Investment ÷ Monthly Savings

          = $12,000 ÷ $1,000
          = 12 months

Scenario Testing

To be fully prepared for questions you will eventually be asked, scenario testing is strongly advised. When you developed your Influence Map in Chapter 6, you documented costs associated with best case, most likely and worst case scenarios. It is also a good idea to develop similar scenarios for the benefits you expect—such as increased sales. Measuring the financial impact of these scenarios will result in a more robust analysis of your idea.

The simplest approach to scenario testing is to analyze the extremes. This includes running the financials as follows:

- Assume every worst case financial impact is encountered;

- Assume every best case financial impact is encountered; and

- Assume all the "most likely" costs are encountered.

You'll know your idea is a good one if it produces benefit even when all of your worst case financials are included. This is not likely, however, so you will also want to determine some level of probability for each of your scenarios. Get input from the stakeholders in each organization regarding their view of the probabilities associated with each scenario.

V. Make a Business Assessment

If you include the right stakeholders in steps I-IV, steps V and VI will likely be superfluous. For Sheri Coppedge, a Director of Alliance Accounts at Marriott International, engaging a host of internal and external customers from the concept stage led the group to commit to a plan by the time the analysis was complete.

Best Practice

"Like most global corporations, one of my customers has a large headquarters building to which its employees often travel. For years, when employees came into town, they stayed in a nearby apartment complex the company owned. Managing an apartment complex was not one of this company's core competencies, and its employees had often expressed their desire to stay at a hotel. As this company's SAM, I was of course very interested in having those travelers stay at Marriott facilities instead!

This was no simple recommendation, however. There was much skepticism within Marriott as to whether my customer would ever be open to utilizing hotels instead of its apartment building. Then, how would we get both independently-owned and franchised hotels to agree to lower contracted rates? There were also systems challenges. Not only were my internal colleagues skeptical, but so was my customer.

To make a long story short, we did win a multi-year contract for a significant number of rooms. We were successful because first of all, I included both my customer and every major Marriott function on the planning team. We mapped every process to determine whether and how we could make this work. Without the functional expertise on the team, it would have been impossible for us to build a complete story. We also succeeded because we conducted in-depth 'what if' financial analyses. This needed to be a 'win' for my client as well as the hotels, and once everyone understood what the break-even points were, they also understood the assumptions that supported the break-even. Lastly, we were able to demonstrate to my customer the value of Marriott taking over this component of their employees' travel needs.

By involving my customer's subject matter experts in the analysis phase, the solution was a 'joint masterpiece.' After the analysis process, there was no selling or negotiating necessary, because it had all been completed during the discovery / analysis phase. I was pleasantly surprised when I realized I would not have to go through a complex process to close the deal!"

Although your ultimate goal is to have all your efforts play out this brilliantly, there will be more times than not that you need to take your business case and "sell" it internally, perhaps to multiple parties with differing agendas. As a salesperson, you have a "glass half full" attitude. In your visionary role, and when you are trying to sell your ideas, you like to communicate the benefits of your proposed solution. But in your role as a businessperson, you have now taken the time to analyze organizational outlays in order to present a fair and accurate analysis. You also understand the financial implications of what you are asking for.

Your goal is to demonstrate balance—you are a customer advocate as well as a company advocate.

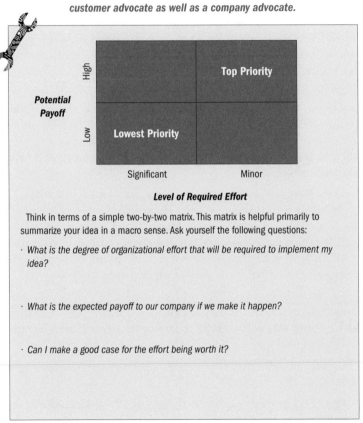

Think in terms of a simple two-by-two matrix. This matrix is helpful primarily to summarize your idea in a macro sense. Ask yourself the following questions:

· *What is the degree of organizational effort that will be required to implement my idea?*

· *What is the expected payoff to our company if we make it happen?*

· *Can I make a good case for the effort being worth it?*

As the matrix suggests, it will be easier for you to sell your idea if it is relatively painless for the organization to implement and the payoff is significant. Before you discard ideas that will require high levels of effort, yet return a low payoff, take the the time to determine whether changes to the idea could result in its migrating to a different cell. For example, is there a way to leverage your idea across multiple customers? If so, the potential payoff could move from low to high. When developing the implementation plan, what ideas were introduced that could require less effort for the organization, yet still result in high payoff?

As a businessperson who must protect your own company's resources, you will recognize the vulnerability of your idea if it falls in the lower left quadrant. If your work to-date suggests this is where it falls, and it is not apparent how you could shift it elsewhere, you must honestly assess whether you should pursue the idea further. Remember that your own credibility is at stake if your idea becomes a costly mistake in your company's archives.

You might find that your worst-case scenario does fall into the lower left quadrant, but that the most likely and best-case scenarios do not. Recognizing that weakness in your idea at this stage gives you a chance to address it now, rather than in a high-stakes meeting with decision-makers.

Let's say you now know that your idea is, in fact, worthy of more attention. At this point, you have a firm handle on the feasibility and benefits of implementation. You have a clear understanding of who will support your idea, as well as who might not and why they might not. It is time for you to present your analysis to the decision-makers.

When there are multiple decision-makers, such as in multiple geographies or business units, be prepared for a series of meetings. As you developed your Influence Map in Chapter 6, you recognized that there are decision-makers for just about every facet of impact your idea creates. You also saw that gaining the support of one decision-maker often led to gaining support from another.

One more thought on all those decision-makers you've outlined: there may also be others that you've not yet uncovered, depending on the culture of your company. After you ask yourself the following questions—you might realize that there are even more individuals to add to your list of meetings;

- *How does change typically happen?*

- *Who has successfully introduced new ideas in the past, and how did they do it?*

- *Are there key people who should be involved, even if their functional responsibilities don't make that apparent?*

VI. Present to the Decision-Makers

The beginning of your agenda for meeting with the people you need to influence will be similar to the presentation you developed in Step II of Chapter 6. It is important to recognize that although you have shared much of this information in the past, not everyone will remember it. You need to get your audience "on the same page" as you, so creating an appropriate focus on the need is critical.

We refer to "presentations" and "audience" as if every meeting is formal, with you standing in the front of a room full of people with your deck of slides. This is often not the format of these meetings. The following agenda can be both an outline of a one-on-one meeting you may have, as well as a formal final presentation that calls for carefully prepared slides.

Agenda
1. Introduce your idea.
2. Why is your idea needed?
3. What is the current base case?
4. Why should your company consider this idea?
5. Outline the impacts relevant to your audience. Be prepared to outline other impacts that your audience might be interested in hearing about.
6. Present your financial rationale.
3. Seek approval

The first four agenda items were described on pages 106-107 of Chapter 6. Beginning with the fifth, the following provides more detail:

5. **Outline the impacts relevant to your audience.** We assume you will be holding a series of presentations, and if you idea is complex you do not need to cover the full extent of your analyses. As with many situations, your audience will want to know "How does this impact me?" Be prepared to discuss your process for determining the impacts, who in this person's organization was involved and any potential weaknesses in your analysis.

   Also be prepared to outline other impacts that your audience might find interesting or relevant. If you have gained the approval of another business unit to revise its customer service processes, that might help your cause with this other particular business unit. In fact, there may be efficiencies gained when you achieve multiple endorsements.

   Think, too, of the LETS Influence process you reviewed in Chapter 7. An important message to convey is the *alignment* you've achieved in your recommendation. You have created a win-win solution, and you want your audience to recognize it as such.

6. **Present your financial rationale.** Depending on your audience, this could be tricky. Even if you have determined that your

proposal is financially sound, there will likely be entities within the corporation for whom this is simply an added expense. For example, increased revenues don't really help the operations manager who has to provide additional training to support the solution. It might even be that an entire business unit or country is being asked to sacrifice profit in order for the corporation to benefit. This has been discussed a couple of times, and we will emphasize it again:

> *If an organization's ability to achieve any of its key results is going to be affected, the most senior executive of that organization will need to be involved. That executive may not be willing (or able) to make the change without approval from his boss, who is likely the president of the division or the CEO of the corporation. Do not expect that you will be able to accomplish what you want without the proper levels of decision-makers involved!*

If you are in such a situation, you should first meet with the executive who has the authority to approve such changes, and present the facts. State clearly that some entities are being asked to sacrifice results in some areas (revenues, profits or expenses), but that the corporation as a whole will benefit. Even the toughest of CEOs should recognize that much can be gained by making appropriate adjustments, usually in the form of a "credit" for what was given up.

7. **Seek approval**. Be clear about what you are asking for. Depending on where you are in your series of presentations, you might be asking for an "OK" to use their buy-in as a means of gaining buy-in from others. That is very different than if you are asking for resources to begin work on the idea. If you are in what (you hope) is the final "go, no-go" presentation, be prepared to describe the time-line of what will happen next.

Escalation: The Advantage of Authority

Although we've already stated that the modern view of leadership is to lead as if one does not have authority, there is no question that the use of authority is often helpful and frequently used. Think of the times your CEO has gotten involved with a sales situation—perhaps a huge revenue opportunity, or an account that was about to cancel. What happened? Chances are that **everyone** pulled out all the stops, and you won the business. Stephanie Fuller, Senior National Account Manager with Office Depot, describes such a scenario:

"Our CEO, Bruce Nelson, believes in the value of involvement with customers. I asked Bruce to contact the CEO of one of my prospects, because

I wanted to get all the different levels talking to each other. I also wanted to establish a corporate relationship that included an exchange of business between the two companies. Following the meeting, Office Depot ousted an incumbent of over ten years!"

The Vision and Strategic Objectives of Your CEO

CEOs juggle two critical elements of business success: They envision the future of tomorrow, and they execute on financial targets today. They must strategize to capture value from the company's current position while creating options to occupy future positions that may have value.

Simple, right? Consider this. There is an inherent tension between these two objectives. Should the company allocate resources to long-term strategic investments, or focus on short-term revenue-generating activities? Should they invest in long-term positioning (launch a new product or open a global market) or manage short-term profitability (clear debt off the balance sheet)? How can they balance both objectives so they can capitalize on the future and thrive today?

Process to Gain Executive Support
· Identify the vision and strategic objective of your CEO.
· Link strategic account performance to the CEO agenda.
· Communicate value to the "C" level.

Copyright © 1998, Visionary Selling.

As you may have already experienced, the current short-term agendas of senior management do not always encourage the long-term view of strategic account management. The CEO of your company is preoccupied with the business of leading the company and the responsibilities of leading its people. These activities can rob him of the ability to keep a long-term perspective about where the company is headed.

Is your recommendation a long-term strategic investment or a short-term revenue-generating activity? Or both? You must demonstrate the long-term strategic value and / or the short-term profitability return in the language senior management uses to evaluate these options everyday—the language of business finance.

When communicating with executives, begin by concentrating on what their concerns are today. The checklist below will help you determine areas of interest to them. Most CEOs will have at least a passing interest in each of the 20 areas listed, and will be intensely interested in several. Your job is to determine which are the most important to them right now. You can use that information as the basis for your communication of the positive impact of SAM on the company's short-term success and long-term results.

20 Areas of Executive Focus
1. PROFITABILITY
2. Return on Assets
3. Return on Invested Capital
4. Economic Value Added (EVA)
5. Balanced Scorecard
6. Productivity / Revenue per Employee
7. Time to Market
8. Asset Management
9. Customer Loyalty / Customer Relationship Management (CRM)
10. Best Practices
11. Intellectual Capital /Patents
12. Brand Management
13. Global Markets
14. Emerging Markets
15. Competitive Pressure
16. Strategic Alliances
17. Mergers & Acquisitions
18. Internet / e-Commerce
19. Outsourcing / Single Sourcing
20. Security

Copyright © 1998, Visionary Selling.

As you consider the list above, think about the following questions in order to link your recommendation to the CEO agenda:

- *Which financial metrics does your company use to measure profitable growth and shareholder value?*

- *How can you demonstrate to your CEO the value of an investment in your recommendation, using his or her criteria and metrics?*

- *How can you establish linkage between your recommendation and your CEO's measures of profitability?*

- *Is the current focus on increasing revenues or decreasing expenses?*

- *How does your financial performance compare to that of your key competitors?*

- *What operational metrics does the company use to manage efficiencies?*

Before you escalate to your CEO or other senior executives, analyze how your recommendation impacts each of the financial and operational metrics used by your company, and design your conversation with their priorities in mind.

Summary

You've now concluded the part of the book aimed at providing tools to you, the SAM. As we stated in the Introduction to Part II, our goal was to enhance your skill level. Regardless of whether you are an experienced SAM, or one who is new to the position, you know that your skills will never "give you authority." Your ability to navigate your way through your own organization in the *absence* of authority should be your focus.

Part III has some important messages for the senior executives in your company. The more they recognize the kinds of things they need to do, which will minimize the barriers you currently encounter, the more efficient you can be. Wouldn't it be great if you could shift some of the time you spend selling internally toward selling to your customer?

In the meantime, prepare one last action plan for yourself:

1. I should become more disciplined about the following steps (check any that apply): ___ Preparing financial analyses ___ Making a "go / no-go" assessment ___ Presenting to decision-makers
2. As I analyze ideas that have been resisted, the following are the ways I did not properly prepare:
3. Situations in which I have seen escalation effectively used: Situations in which I have seen escalation not effectively used: I will improve my own use of escalation by:
4. In general, I can enhance my abilities to influence internally by:

PART III
The Management Mandate

Part III:
The Mangement Mandate

Part II of this book focused on skills and tools for the strategic account manager. This framework for SAMs was presented as a way to work with, and even around, the inherent organizational barriers that exist inside their companies because breaking down or removing those barriers is not typically within the purview of a SAM. That is not to say that those barriers need not be addressed! They are, in fact, the most stubborn, complex, pervasive factor standing in the way of true customer focus, as evidenced by a recent SAMA study that highlights the gaps between high and low performing SAM programs. That is why Part III of this book is so critical. It will focus on the role senior management must play in removing the organizational obstacles that impede effective strategic account management.

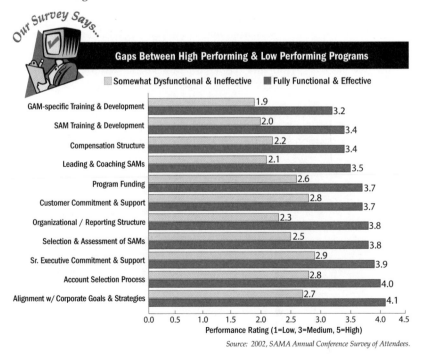

Source: 2002, SAMA Annual Conference Survey of Attendees.

Chapter 9 provides guidance to "sales leadership" in developing organizational competencies to support SAM initiatives. In recognition of the variety of sales management roles that exist in firms, we are intentionally using a broad term to refer to those responsible for some aspect of key customer strategy overall. You may have divisional oversight, geographical oversight, industry oversight or even shared responsibility within a SAM program that is a true corporate overlay. Regardless of your title or scope of responsibility, we will refer to you, the targeted reader of this chapter, as the strategic account management (SAM) "Program Director." Basically, if you can help to break down the barriers that cause SAMs to spend so much energy "selling internally," this chapter is addressed to you!

We will challenge you to ask yourself "does our organization make it easier for SAMs to be effective? Or does it ignore the barriers that cause SAMs to say the 'internal sell' is the toughest part of their job?"

When we look at an organization's readiness for strategic account management, we will look at the following aspects:

- Is senior management committed to the program? This includes both resource allocation as well as a willingness to address and resolve conflicting objectives across organizational silos.

- Are roles and responsibilities well defined?

- Are the "silos" well informed about, and aligned with, the strategic accounts program? Do they understand how they will be asked to contribute to its success?

- Does the company's infrastructure enable on-time and quality delivery of products / services? Do its systems contribute to knowledge sharing and provide the information that SAMs need?

Consider the following chart as you think about your own organization's readiness for strategic account management:

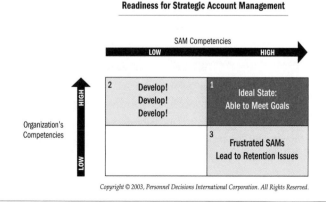

Readiness for Strategic Account Management

Copyright © 2003, Personnel Decisions International Corporation. All Rights Reserved.

1. When both the organization and the SAMs are well developed, this is the ideal state. The ability to meet goals, oftentimes including strong growth, can be expected.

2. If the organization is ready, but its SAMs are not, development of the SAMs is the required solution (assuming you've selected correctly on criteria such as traits and their overall potential to be successful). Development can take place in many ways, including training, mentoring, shadowing experienced SAMs and coaching.

3. This is a scenario that can lead to frustrated SAMs. At best, frustrated SAMs are less productive than they could be, and at worst they leave your company or leave their position. Good SAMs are highly talented individuals. Shame on you if you lose them because your organization creates too many barriers.

The scenario that you, as an executive, need to be most concerned about is having SAMs who are capable of performing well in their job, but an organization that is not ready.

As a SAM Program Director, you have some leverage to rectify the processes (or lack thereof) that are standing in the way of efficient, productive (translate: more profitable) relationships with your key customers. But the reality is that your leverage is simply not enough to truly build institutional relationships. The true point of leverage resides within the Executive Suite—a place devoid of silo loyalty, possessing a broader view and a long-term vision. **Chapter 10** delivers you a tool to "influence up" in your organization on behalf of the SAM program, and more importantly, the customer.

Setting aside the obvious reality that CEOs are pressured by the short-term performance climate we are all dealing with, the CEO is where the buck stops, and most of them are keen to identify the inefficiencies inside their own organization. In this chapter, the responsibility of the Executive Suite in enabling customer focus is made abundantly clear in a direct manner backed up by compelling quantitative and qualitative evidence. Our aim is to help you convince your CEO that your own organizational processes and structures are inhibiting customer focus, derailing superior delivery of good and services and inhibiting innovation. Armed with this information, and some serious homework on your firm's particular challenges, you will be better positioned to make a strong business case inside your company for fixing these issues.

We've written this chapter directly to your CEO, even providing a stand-alone version of **Chapter 10** so that you can hand it to your top decision-makers as opposed to handing them this entire book.* We also realize that you may prefer to absorb the argument yourself and find less direct ways of filtering it where it needs to go inside your organization. How you decide to utilize this chapter will depend entirely on the role you play within your company, the degree of management support your firm currently enjoys and the amount of risk you are willing and able to take in order to make strategic account management an Executive Suite priority.

* A copy of the stand-alone **Message to the CEO** *was originally included with this book. If you'd like another one, please contact SAMA at 312-251-3131.*

Chapter 9:
Removing Organizational Obstacles: The Role of Sales Management

 "Everybody will tell you that global account management is an idea whose time has come, but not everybody wants to invest in it. Our compensation, recognition and organizational structures do not contribute to globalization. To get the resources I need is like pulling teeth because our organizational structure is geographical. I can tell people the account is billing three billion dollars a year with our company and that this is what the customer wants. They say, 'I understand all that stuff and it's good for our corporation but I am paid and judged on how much money I make. Why should I pay for my people to go on customer calls to the U.K. when I don't get any benefit from what they sell there?'"

THIS IS WHERE YOU COME IN!

Organizational issues like those mentioned above are common roadblocks to successful execution of SAM strategy. When left unaddressed, they not only contribute to missed opportunities, but pose serious threats to the security of your key customer relationships. In some cases, management has concluded that the failure to see a return on the significant investment made in strategic account management is because the strategy itself is flawed. But if you're reading this, you know that is not where the problem resides. It is the *implementation* of SAM strategies that most firms struggle with, and given the massive shift required to focus your entire organization outwardly on the customer, it isn't a surprise.

There are a variety of actions an organization can take to foster an environment in which the SAM, as well as the SAM strategy, can best function. This chapter addresses what you, as leader of a strategic accounts program, can and must do to resolve, or at least minimize, the primary obstacles that confront today's complex, matrixed organizations.

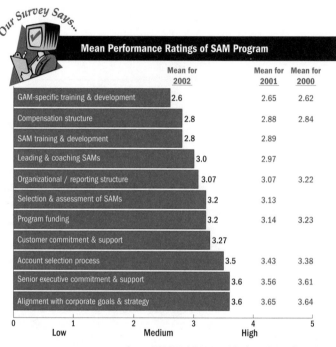

Mean Performance Ratings of SAM Program

	Mean for 2002	Mean for 2001	Mean for 2000
GAM-specific training & development	2.6	2.65	2.62
Compensation structure	2.8	2.88	2.84
SAM training & development	2.8	2.89	
Leading & coaching SAMs	3.0	2.97	
Organizational / reporting structure	3.07	3.07	3.22
Selection & assessment of SAMs	3.2	3.13	
Program funding	3.2	3.14	3.23
Customer commitment & support	3.27		
Account selection process	3.5	3.43	3.38
Senior executive commitment & support	3.6	3.56	3.61
Alignment with corporate goals & strategy	3.6	3.65	3.64

```
0            1            2            3            4            5
           Low                      Medium                   High
```

Source: 2000-2002, SAMA Annual Conference Survey of Attendees.

As the chart above shows, even the best organizations perform well below their potential across all SAM program elements. There's good news embedded in those statistics—not only are you not alone in the challenges you grapple with, but your ability to make incremental improvements in these areas can give your company a significant advantage over your competitors.

Whereas this book previously focused on *skills* for the SAM, this chapter focuses on *strategies* for you. The four we will discuss are:

- Gaining the **commitment** of senior executives in your company to the strategic accounts program;

- Managing your human resources for optimum performance, beginning with defining **roles and responsibilities**, so that everyone understands the contributions expected of them, and then ensuring you have the **right talent** to fulfill those roles;

- Creating **alignment** across the various entities within your company, such as functions, geographies and business units; and

- Ensuring that the **information infrastructure** not only supports the efficient delivery of basic customer requirements, but also fosters a knowledge-based environment that enables value creation.

Executive Commitment

Does this sound like your company?

"The procurement manager for one of our top accounts told me that one of our general managers was refusing to serve two of their remote offices. As Director of National Accounts, I visited the general manager and found out he was purposefully ignoring the account because it was unprofitable for him. Subsequently, our CEO picked up the phone and sent a distribution voicemail to all general managers, saying, 'We are in the national accounts business. Your jobs are to service the field locations of national accounts. And if you don't get it, call me right now.' Needless to say, the phone never rang. It's very important to be able to play that card if necessary."

If it does, congratulations! Though you'll still have your work cut out for you, your job will be infinitely easier if you work in a company where you are *"able to play that card if necessary."* It's no wonder that SAMA members are nearly unanimous in their agreement that a SAM program must be mandated from the top to truly achieve results. Executive commitment, participation and visibility are necessary to

"The key to success in this program is always with senior management. The vision of what we are doing with the global accounts has to be communicated clearly and forcefully. Otherwise, the day-to-day selling activities in the field will take precedence."

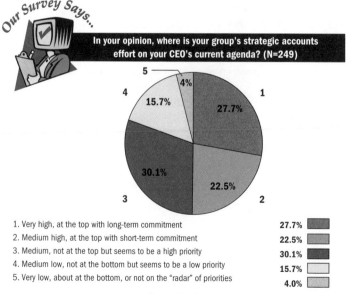

Our Survey Says...

In your opinion, where is your group's strategic accounts effort on your CEO's current agenda? (N=249)

- 1: 27.7%
- 2: 22.5%
- 3: 30.1%
- 4: 15.7%
- 5: 4%

1. Very high, at the top with long-term commitment — 27.7%
2. Medium high, at the top with short-term commitment — 22.5%
3. Medium, not at the top but seems to be a high priority — 30.1%
4. Medium low, not at the bottom but seems to be a low priority — 15.7%
5. Very low, about at the bottom, or not on the "radar" of priorities — 4.0%

Source: 2002, SAMA Annual Conference Survey of Attendees.

garner resources and to establish the authority of the program. It is very challenging to get approval for ideas that require reallocating business units' revenue or spending capital dollars without executive support. Driving strategic account management through the organization will be greatly facilitated if communications are accompanied by a strong message from the CEO.

While a strong CEO advocate creates considerable advantage, the reality of today's business environment indicates there are no guarantees that your CEO will continue his or her support over time. Whether it's pressure from Wall Street, a failing economy, a corporate merger or even leadership change at the top, there are powerful forces in play that have caused many well-supported programs to stall, digress or even disband with incredible speed. For this reason, your role in reinforcing what backing you have, and leveraging it while you have it, is still a critical one.

The most powerful tool you can use in gaining and maintaining top executive support for SAM initiatives is a strong business case. Remember that your company is not an endless pool of resources. When you stake a claim to a portion of those resources, you're not only up against a number of others seeking to do the same, but you are likely competing against solid ideas backed by well-developed rationales. Although the tools provided in Chapters 3 through 8 were presented in the context of SAMs marshalling resources, the model for achieving IMPACT Without Authority is applicable to you as well as you "sell up" within your firm.

Bottom line, you need to think of top executive support as an ongoing journey rather than a destination. Even if your strategic accounts program is already established, it can be difficult to get others in your organization to respond to the needs of strategic accounts unless they know it's a strategy actively supported by senior management. Effectively using your executive advocates to create additional executive advocates across your firm helps build *institutional* commitment that is more likely to survive the various threats that we outlined earlier.

"There's share of wallet and then there's share of mind. The sponsor's role is not to manage the account. It is to win the mind of the client. The account team will manage the wallet."

Developing Executive Sponsors

Adopting a systematic, focused approach to executive sponsorship has proven to be a hallmark of both success and longevity of strategic account programs. Because the stakes are high, you might not get a second chance to "get it right." The first critical task is deciding what will work in your company. Like so many other aspects of strategic account management, benchmarking general practices is a good place to start, but carefully selecting the features that will fit into your unique environment is key. While the features of executive sponsorship programs vary from company to company, the primary determinant of success lies in clarity around the initiative. The most common missteps occur from the outset, when goals, objectives, roles and responsibilities are not clearly articulated and communicated across various stakeholders.

Choosing your sponsors carefully is a critical success factor stressed by many SAMA members who have gone through this process. What you want is a combination of vision *and* enthusiasm—one without the other will be ineffective at best, and lethal in the worst case.

Strive to formalize the executive sponsor's role, even to the point of including it in the executive's job description and performance criteria. As you define it, think in terms of the following areas of responsibility of an executive sponsor:

- Customer-related: the sponsor is a relationship-builder. With the SAM's input, sponsors will develop their own relationships in the account as well as help SAMs penetrate higher levels more quickly than they could on their own.

- Internal: the sponsor is both a customer and account team advocate. Since many of the issues presented in this book involve barriers, the executive should help the SAM and the team to navigate and break down some of those barriers.

- Team: the sponsor is also a participating account team member. This includes being a coach to the team and helping it shape its priorities to support corporate priorities.

Unfortunately, reports of executive sponsors "taking over" client management are not as rare as you would think. It is important to explain up front that their role is to *support* the sales process, not be part of it. They should operate at the highest level within the client organization, enhancing the credibility of the account team by demonstrating support for the relationship.

Finding the right "fit" between sponsor and account is another key success factor that cannot be stressed enough. If you are just establishing the role of executive sponsor, think about the strategic priorities of each account. Suggest that these priorities be considered when matching executives to the various accounts. For example, if an account is growing fast and your company will benefit from that growth, an executive sponsor who can materially contribute to the achievement of that growth would be advantageous. That might be a functional executive in manufacturing, or it might be a business unit leader or country manager whose products could experience increased sales. Again, you want the account's goals to become their

---

goals. Other criteria to consider when matching sponsors to accounts include identifying where relationships already exist, determining where skills of the sponsor might complement the skills of the SAM, and identifying accounts for which the potential sponsors have particular interests.

The Executive Sponsor in Action

A strategic relationship with a customer requires buy-in at the strategic level, and the executive level is where strategy is formulated. When account executives sell into operations or mid-level management, the account is often served just the same as any other account, despite being labeled "strategic" account management. A SAM can be more effective at selling to the executive level with the participation of his or her own executives.

Another valuable role for your executive sponsor to play is to help navigate the political landscape within your customer's organization. For example, an executive can assist in providing political recognition to deserving customer personnel at the request of the account manager. To impart such visibility is a great approach for gaining or building momentum for a specific cause. When account managers find themselves politically blocked by someone in the customer's organization, an executive sponsor can often assist. By virtue of stature, an executive has permission to go places that may be seen as politically out of bounds for the account manager. Finally, a well-schooled and well-informed executive can assist the account manager in executing a plan to start or advance an internal customer power struggle that is designed for the displacement of a competitor. An account manager would find this very difficult to accomplish by himself, especially if the power struggle takes place across multiple levels and departments within the customer organization.

Even more powerful is if your SAMs can leverage the power of CEO involvement in everyday sales situations, instead of utilizing it only in dramatic situations with gigantic stakes and a high profile. David Macaulay from Siemens describes how his company achieves this:

"I have five bosses in my position as Senior Vice President and Managing Director at Siemens. I report to one of six board members on the Central Board, and to four Business Unit CEOs who fund the Key Accounts program. The program was created to exploit the power of the Siemens brand. Before the key accounts program was initiated, each group would go independently to a company without understanding what other groups were doing. This created conflict in the mind of the customer and led to decreased productivity and missed opportunities.

My team of 30 KAMs directs all the people in operations worldwide that handle the account. They have no authority to set plans, incent or hire and fire. What they do have is a charter from the Chairman of the Board that says they are responsible for worldwide strategy, planning and leadership of the customer. Everyone knows that each KAM reports through me to the Board; it was set up this way so people would recognize that the KAM is 'close to God.' The response to the program has also created an informal charter from the customer, who now demands 'one team' from Siemens."

Utilizing executives in a focused way with your strategic accounts typically generates increased customer commitment and strategic-level conversations. In addition to taking your executives into customer organizations, the following ideas bring your customers into your company.

Customer Councils

An effective strategy for communicating issues and opportunities to your senior management team is the use of customer councils. A customer council is a group of customers brought together to both learn and offer feedback. Such councils can be scheduled as a stand-alone event, or they might be held in conjunction with some other event, such as an industry conference.

Typically held annually, key customers are invited to hear about and discuss topics relevant to your business relationship. In determining who to invite, it is important to first clearly define your objectives for the council. If you want the meeting to be focused on high-level strategy, invite senior executives. If you want to get input on specifications or micro issues, invite customers who can provide that level of input to you. If the meeting is to be strategic in nature, your CEO, or at least the president of your division, should host the meeting and issue the invitation. You will attract higher-level executives if your own top executives will also be there. One objective for this kind of meeting might be to get feedback on the degree to which your customers see your strategy as aligned with their needs. Another could be to share information about how the CEO envisions future change – e.g., a merger or regulatory changes – will impact your industry and your customers. Your invitation to be a part of the council should address how the attendees will benefit.

Jim Bierfeldt, Vice President of Marketing for USCO Logistics, established an annual customer council in 1998 as a means to help validate its corporate strategy. In addition to that, Jim has seen the council enhance overall business relationships with key clients. He also cites customers influencing USCO's senior executives as a benefit. "Having our most important customers tell us that integrating information systems was their most acute pain point was key to our management team recognizing that systems integration must be an absolute priority for our company."

If the meeting is more tactical, the host should be a senior executive who has responsibility over a key area of focus that impacts the attendees. For example, if you want to get input on promotional activities that will impact your customers, include the executives who have planning and implementation responsibilities for them. Invite customers who are involved with this level of their business.

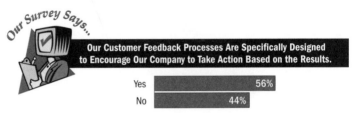

Our Customer Feedback Processes Are Specifically Designed to Encourage Our Company to Take Action Based on the Results.

Yes	56%
No	44%

Source: 2001, Survey on Leading-Edge Practices for Measuring & Managing Customer Loyalty, SAMA, PDI, IMPAX.

Customer Advisory Boards

Whereas an annual council tends to be an "event", a more ongoing means of weaving the customer into your organization is through customer advisory boards. Since advisory boards require long-term commitment from senior executives, you might assume that companies that create them are already attuned enough to the customer that the SAM's ability to influence is high. This is not necessarily so. In many organizations, we see the CEO / President and the Sales VP sponsoring the advisory board, with the functional VPs not as enthusiastic. It is those functional VPs who, once they get more involved with the input provided by the advisory board, become stronger advocates.

The primary objective for establishing a customer advisory board is to learn how the company can better serve, and communicate with, its most strategic customers. Similar to a customer council, it can also serve as a sounding board for new ideas and for validating strategy. They often get beyond strategy as well, for example, by helping to define communications and marketing plans. Board members generally serve a two or three-year term, sometimes on a rotating schedule, so that not all members are replaced at the same time. The advisory board meets two to four times per year, with a well-defined agenda for each meeting.

The "fear factor" sometimes prevents organizations from establishing a customer advisory board. Executives don't want the meetings to turn into complaint sessions—or worse, to create expectations that cannot be met. A one-time council is an easier way to start. The level of commitment is not defined at the start, and if your company feels it cannot continue the event, it is not something that has to be "undone" or discontinued.

Similar to the council, clearly define your objectives and let that drive who to invite. The advisory board should be small enough that in-depth discussions are easily facilitated, but large enough to still be effective despite missing members due to the complexities of schedules.

Leadership Team Meetings

Perhaps your organization does not feel it is ready for either a customer advisory board or council. Another method of bringing the customer closer to your executive team is to establish an agenda item on its quarterly planning meetings consisting of a customer coming in to make a presentation. This is an excellent approach for helping your executives learn more about strategic customers, and it helps those customers be heard at the highest levels of your organization. It also gives recognition and a voice to the SAMs who are managing those relationships.

As one executive whose company implemented this explained,

"We were finding that our quarterly meetings were becoming more administrative than anything else, and we needed to remind ourselves that the reason we exist is for our customers!"

You will need to plan who will be invited to present well in advance. Because it is an executive meeting, choose an appropriately high-level customer to enable peer-to-peer interaction. Throughout the course of the year, have a variety of industries or product lines represented. Although you should include customers with whom you have both solid and struggling relationships, it is always best to start with someone with whom the relationship is more positive. The executive team will feel more comfortable with this as a start (although you should prepare them to hear some constructive criticism as well!). In addition, if the relationship is too weak, the customer might not feel comfortable providing feedback to a large group of executives. Depending on the reasons for the declining relationship, they might feel like they are being put "on the spot."

Your customer is being asked to present, but that does not mean they should have to present a formal set of slides (although they probably will). Simply talking will be quite powerful. The agenda for what your customer will talk about might include the following:

Agenda

- An introduction on the customer's organization, including their mission, values and strategic direction.

- How and why the decision was made to buy from your company, and how they are using your company's products and services.

- Key success factors in the relationship. This information will, in effect, highlight what is important to them and will reinforce to your executive team strengths that can and should be leveraged.

- Challenges or obstacles they perceive your company will face when working with them in the future. Again, this will highlight what is of prime importance to your customer.

There are also some cautions that should be outlined:

- Be sure the account manager who is responsible for this customer account is present in the meeting. It makes the customer more comfortable when they see a familiar face. In addition, the SAM needs to hear the discussion first-hand, and it would appear odd to the customer if he were not there.

- As with all executive interactions with the customer, your company's leaders need to be coached about not making promises! In fact, this is an excellent time to remind them that they can be most effective if they acknowledge the SAM's role and defer questions as appropriate to them for answering either then or later. The SAM's worst nightmare is to have worked on something for months, only to have an executive make an off-hand promise that either negates that work or creates higher expectations than will be delivered.

- Do not expect customers to give you a detailed analysis of every strength and weakness that your company has. Remember that their focus is similar to that of your executive team: impact on business results, not necessarily the tactical details of day-to-day interactions.

The overall aim in engaging executives is to facilitate the alignment of your company with your customers' business objectives. As a SAM Program Director, you must take the lead in establishing and maintaining effective executive involvement. If done well, you will be providing assistance to your SAMs in overcoming many of their main challenges such as acquisition of resources, formulation of account strategy, dispute resolution and opening doors in the client organization.

Talent Implications

Defining Roles and Responsibilities Across the Organization

Understanding what needs to get done for the customer and deciding how best to make that happen inside your company is the foundation for strategic talent management. This is why thoroughly and clearly defining roles and responsibilities regarding both selling and relationship management is so critical to success—where you land will either help or hinder a SAM's ability to work across your organization. As one VP described the problem:

"Unfortunately, we are organized in a manner to be decentralized at the customer level, the local level. The individual business units (BU) organization is not best suited to handling national and global customers. People who are running those BUs or working in those BUs are so focused on what happens within the walls of their compound that it's difficult sometimes to have them do something for the greater good. That's why we have GAMs. It's really to overcome that compartmentalization. You lose your power as you fragment your organization in its face to the customer. There goes your value-add and the power that you bring to the relationship."

The template below is useful when planning the details of "who does what." Use a different worksheet for the following activities; you might determine other activities that need the same levels of role definition.

1. Activity: Business Development

2. Activity: Managing Customer Relationships

3. Activity: Servicing the Account

4. Activity: Developing Account Strategy

5. Activity: Managing the Contractual Relationship

Strategic Account Management: Roles & Responsibilities

Activity: _____

SAM	Field Sales
Operations	Senior Management / Executive Sponsor

To fill in the squares on the grid, ask the following questions:

- *How will this function (e.g., the SAM, field-level sales, etc.) be directly involved in this activity?*

- *How will this function support this activity?*

- *What should the function communicate, and to whom?*

- *How can this function help any of the other functions?*

- *What uncertainties exist? i.e., is there something that is unclear or confusing?*

1. 35.8 % Combine into one position the three functions of a) servicing existing customers, b) growing more business with existing key customers and c) targeting potential new key customers.

2. 43.2 % Separate the above into two different positions of a) servicing and growing existing key customers and b) targeting potential new key customers.

3. 15.5% Separate into three different positions of a) servicing existing key customers, b) growing more business with existing key customers and c) targeting new key customers.

4. 5.4% Other

Source: 2002, Survey of Strategic Account Management Compensation Practices, SAMA, The Alexander Group Inc.

Account Teams

When defining roles and responsibilities, another decision you will face is whether to establish formal account teams. Well-run teams will engage more cross-functional, cross-divisional and / or cross-regional employees in growing the customer account. It is easier to establish accountabilities for the account's success when a formal team is in place, and your SAMs will definitely find it easier to navigate the rest of the organization with team members in place to guide them. It is also easier to work through the details of roles and responsibilities when a team is charged with making it work.

Richard Wilder at Iron Mountain believes you must match your internal resources with customer structure. Iron Mountain went through numerous acquisitions to bring a "single face, single solution" to customers but then faced the challenge of providing consistency with decentralized operations in 70 markets running on multiple systems, many having local customization of service offerings.

The solution was to give customers the consistency they wanted through additional support people on the account team who are matched like function to like function. An additional benefit was that the NAM who used to get bogged down in implementing and fixing things at the program owner level is now focused on building the relationship at the senior level. According to Richard, "The NAM used to be pulled down and never pulled up; once you drop down in a relationship it is very hard to get back up."

Why don't all companies establish formal teams? Limited resources—either people or expense. In addition, formal teams are not needed for every strategic account.

The key driver for creating teams should be that the increased interaction and accountabilities associated with a formal team are necessary to achieving the goals for that account.

If a formal team is not needed, don't create one. Successful teaming takes time, especially in the beginning. Although the time is paid for as the team's efforts generate financial results, teams are an investment in their earliest days. Therefore, teams should be used where the payoff will be the greatest to achieve the highest ROI.

Strategic Talent Management:
The Right People in the Right Jobs at the Right Time

Do any of the following scenarios describe your company?

- You start your program with a certain number of SAMs, and 12 to 18 months later it's apparent that only half of them are performing at the level that you need them to be.

- You want to grow your SAM program – and you have accounts that would benefit from having a devoted SAM – but you just don't have people who are ready to move into these new positions.

- Some of your SAMs are ready for a different assignment, but you have no one to backfill them if they move on.

- You spend a lot of money relocating sales people from the field to become strategic account managers, and all too often the SAMs get frustrated in their new position and opt to return back to the field.

- Your company is merging with another and there is no predefined approach to determining which SAMs will be assigned to which accounts.

At the May 2002 SAMA Annual Conference, in a session that was presented on this subject, it was confirmed that organizations are struggling with having SAM positions filled with the "right people at the right time." At one point, participants were asked "How many of you have all your SAM positions filled with the talent you need, and you're developing bench strength for the future?" *No one* raised his or her hand. They were then asked, "How many of you would say you have three-quarters of the positions filled with the talent you need?" Perhaps one-fourth of the audience raised their hands. You get the picture.

This reflects a shift in what organizations see as their primary concern when it comes to their strategic account management programs. In years past, when many companies were first considering implementing strategic account management, their concern was in how to organize the program itself. Now, filling their SAM positions with the talent they need is the primary concern.

Anytime a wrong person is put into a SAM position it's expensive. Costs incurred include training, opportunity costs (i.e., missed opportunities that someone better would have developed), the morale costs of other people working with a low performer, the management costs of spending extra time trying to develop the person and perhaps even recruiting costs.

"Strategic talent management" is simply the organizational planning activities that ensure companies have the right people in the right job at the right time.

It includes both choosing people correctly for specific positions and building bench strength so that the organization is ready for future growth or change.

What *Is* the Profile of a Successful SAM?

When people are placed in a position, many factors affect whether these people will succeed or fail (setting aside organizational issues—a different article is needed to address those). PDI's research has identified six components to be the primary determinants of one's success in a role (see Figure 1 below). We refer to these as the "building blocks of performance." They provide a framework for making decisions about whom to place in a particular position. To most effectively place individuals in a SAM position, therefore, the objective should be to learn as much as possible about the person from these six different perspectives.

Looking at these building blocks, the bottom row includes those factors that are the most difficult to develop in a person and therefore should be used as the minimum criteria for selection into the role. For example, if a job requires a certain level of intelligence, you wouldn't hire someone who is lacking in that area and expect him / her to develop in it. Or, if a person were not motivated to succeed in a position, it would be difficult for him or her to develop an appropriate level of interest in the job.

Figure 1: The Building Blocks of Performance

Copyright © 2002, Personnel Decisions International Corporation. All Rights Reserved.

The upper-level blocks, ideally, would also see a close fit between the person and the position. However, in their absence they can be more easily developed than the lower level blocks. For example, functional skills can be developed, and people can be provided with critical learning experiences.

For high-impact positions, however, it is preferable that the person be "ready now" for the role versus "ready in a year or more, but demonstrates great potential for success." The implications of putting a person into a job with the expectation that he / she will develop the key requisite skills need to be determined. For example, when a company hires a new CEO, it doesn't look for a candidate who has "great potential" and will develop well into the position. It wants a CEO who is "ready now." The same holds true with SAM positions. If a company practices "strategic talent management," it is looking ahead to what its future needs will be and creating development plans for individuals so that its future needs for SAMs can be met with people who are ready for the job.

Expanding on each building block of performance, the following are criteria that PDI has built into its model for appropriate placement in a SAM position:

1. The first component is **cognitive abilities**. In general, cognitive tests are used to measure the prospective SAM's propensity for inductive and deductive reasoning. SAMs must be able to recognize patterns and draw appropriate conclusions for activities such as developing integrated solutions for customer problems, creating a business case, anticipating customer needs and seeing opportunities for change that others might not recognize. Scoring high in deductive reasoning is related to strategic and visionary thinking, which is, of course, an important competency related to SAM success.

2. More often than with cognitive abilities, there is a lack of fit between an individual and the SAM position in the area of **personality traits and work style behaviors**. A large proportion of SAMs have been promoted from a sales position, yet when the profiles of successful field sales reps are compared against those of successful strategic account managers, some key differences in personality and work style traits become apparent. For example, the most successful field sales reps typically enjoy the autonomy of their position, the well-defined processes that support their position and the feeling that they exclusively own the customer relationship. These traits do not work in a strategic account manager's favor! SAMs need to be comfortable working across boundaries and through others, must be patient with a long sales cycle (both externally and internally) and must be able to motivate a cross-functional team toward a common goal. And if your SAM is a GAM, he or she must have a sincere interest in understanding and working in cultures different from their own.

3. What **motivates** employees can be key to their fit in the SAM position. SAMs need to enjoy breaking new ground. They need to be flexible and view the frustrations inherent in the position as challenges. Successful SAMs are characterized as having high aspirations, initiative and high standards of performance. They are also typically self-starters and self-directed.

4 and 5. Companies and employees alike should maintain an inventory of each candidate's **educational background, experiences and accomplishments**. This information is fairly easily obtained. What's not always done well, however, is an

> "Hard driving, quota-based, experienced salespeople don't always fit well into a strategic account management position. I have a few of those people and they get real jittery real quick when they can't close a sale every day or every week."

Figure 2: The Profilor® for Sales Wheel

Key Account Manager

Build Strategic Customer Relationships
Understand Customer Needs
Create Effective Solutions
Professional Knowledge
Demonstrate Adaptability
Customer Factor
Business Knowledge
Credibility and Trust
Self Management Factor
Business / Market Factor
Financial Acumen
The PROFILOR®
Key Account Manager
Improve Processes
Administration Factor
Communication Factor
Communicate Effectively
Leadership Factor
Present with Impact
Plan and Organize
Negotiate Effectively
Influence Without Authority
Lead the Team
Demonstrate Courage and Confidence
Composite: Overall Sales Performance

analysis of what it took to achieve those accomplishments. It is important to understand the competencies and traits that contributed to success in a candidate's educational and work accomplishments and then determine if they are relevant to the SAM position. Several errors can be made when it is assumed that a person's past successes will be repeated in their new assignment. Those past successes are relevant only if the key drivers of success are similar.

Successful SAMs work well with ambiguity. They become creative – versus paralyzed – by a lack of structure. If individuals have only held positions in which high levels of structure and process were present, it cannot be inferred how they will deal with the vagaries of being a SAM. On the other hand, individuals who helped launch a new division or a new product have demonstrated their ability to work in an undefined environment.

Regarding educational background, PDI has found that holding an MBA is a requirement for the SAM position in many corporations. Supplemental education focused on financial acumen is typically either required or provided.

6. The final component, which resides at the top of the "building blocks of performance" is **competencies** or demonstrated skill sets. Most organizations do focus on this category; however, it is often at the expense of the other, equally critical categories. The list of competencies identified by PDI is the result of its research focused specifically on the SAM position (see Figure 2 on page 181).

What Happens When You Don't Consider Critical Factors?

Perhaps you think it's too complicated to consider all six of the factors (see Figure 1 on page 179) when you're considering candidates within your own company. After all, you know who is going to perform well, right?

We see wrong decisions made for a variety of reasons. Managers make decisions based on levels of success in the candidate's past, but the SAM position is likely to be a very different position than any that the candidate has already held.

Have you ever seen the wrong person placed in a job because of one of the following?

- **The Peter Principle:** Getting promoted beyond the level of an individual's competence.

- **Halos and horns:** The assumption that individuals who perform well in one area will perform well in all areas. Or, conversely, if they are not talented in some areas, they won't perform well in the SAM position.

- **Self-cloning:** We all want people who are like ourselves.

- **Myopia:** Too narrow a range of selection criteria is used in the process of placing someone in a job.

- **Varying and subjective standards:** The multiple people involved in a selection process reach divergent conclusions on a person's potential.

- **Writing off individuals:** Not enough is known about an individual, or perhaps an individual has had a recent misstep that contradicts his or her potential.

Matching SAMs to Accounts

When looking at the complete picture of the "ideal SAM," you will notice that it is quite comprehensive—perhaps recommending more than can be easily found in one person. Therefore, it is helpful to understand how to recognize the strongest differentiators between average success and high achievement.

To start, not all SAM positions will require strengths in the same areas. An account that is stable and that has been penetrated deeply requires a different SAM profile than an account in which major opportunities for growth are present. Some accounts might also require a different level of cross-organization work than others. Outline the major goals for each account and, from this outline, determine the talent you will need to achieve those goals. This will help you understand where compromises from the "ideal SAM" might be made.

Once you have a firm understanding of the profile you are seeking, start with the bottom level of the "building blocks." Remember, you run the risk of major difficulties if you compromise on these. Be sure that what motivates your SAM candidate is consistent with the demands of the position. Recognize the traits your SAM will need to meet the demands of working in your organization.

In terms of competencies, one of the strongest differentiators between the most and least successful SAMs is the "lead the team" competency. A candidate's skill level in this area is important to assess because many candidates have had experience with leading direct reports but not in leading a cross-functional group of professionals. "Influencing others" is also a differentiating skill. To accurately determine the competencies in which a candidate is strong, PDI recommends using both structured, behaviorally-based interviews and job simulations that reflect a SAM's true day-in-the-life. Unless a person has obtained objective feedback from others, self-reporting of strengths is not usually correct.

Organizations spend a lot of time strategizing their future vision and how they will compete in the marketplace. They tend not to spend sufficient time strategizing about their future talent needs. "Developing people" activities often drop to the bottom of the priority list, and the effects of this neglect are felt when companies try to fill the critical strategic account manager position.

Filling all of your SAM positions with the talent you need, and having confidence that you have bench strength developing for the future, will only happen by putting in place a comprehensive talent planning process. Identifying employees who have the desire and potential to be a SAM in the future, and then working with them to create an appropriate development plan, will prepare your organization for growth in this job function.

Alignment

In order to gain a competitive advantage, your company must position the relationship with your customers at the core of your corporate strategy. To execute that strategy requires alignment around customers from all parts of the organization, primarily because strong alignment is a key enabler of effective collaboration. As a Program Director, if fostering a collaborative culture isn't currently a top priority, it should be. We have found that firms with a highly collaborative culture can provide a major business differential against competitors, not only by offering the means to be highly responsive to the customer, but through their ability to leverage the collective capability of the firm in order to be innovative. Conversely, lack of effective collaboration impedes an organization's ability to meet time-to-market constraints, affects bottom line costs and minimizes top line profitability.

As recent SAMA data shows, there are many obstacles to internal alignment. Your role as the SAM Program Director is to do whatever you can to eliminate or minimize those obstacles that are standing in the way of greater success with strategic customers. This section will focus on two major culprits of misalignment that most firms are grappling with today—turf issues and compensation conflicts.

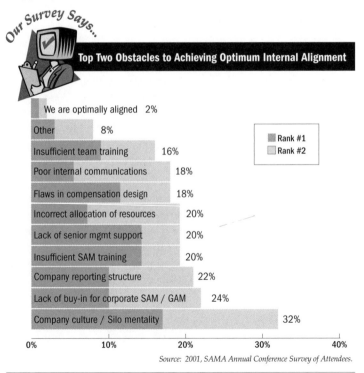

Our Survey Says...

Top Two Obstacles to Achieving Optimum Internal Alignment

- We are optimally aligned 2%
- Other 8%
- Insufficient team training 16%
- Poor internal communications 18%
- Flaws in compensation design 18%
- Incorrect allocation of resources 20%
- Lack of senior mgmt support 20%
- Insufficient SAM training 20%
- Company reporting structure 22%
- Lack of buy-in for corporate SAM / GAM 24%
- Company culture / Silo mentality 32%

Rank #1
Rank #2

0%   10%   20%   30%   40%

Source: 2001, SAMA Annual Conference Survey of Attendees.

Your Role in Minimizing Turf Issues

Because turf issues frequently occur or are reinforced at a high level within a silo, escalation beyond the scope of a SAM is often necessary. As a Program Director, one of the most important roles you can play is to help dismantle and minimize turf issues that stand in the way of what's best for the customer. In some instances, you will have the authority you need to intervene, but in many cases you will need to navigate the internal politics of your company in search of a resolution. Whatever the circumstance, you will increase your success rate if you take time to accurately diagnose the origin of the conflict. **Chapter 1** highlighted the primary sources of turf battles. This list merits repeating for emphasis:

- *Resources:* In a climate of shrinking resources, entities often end up competing against one another for a piece of the limited pie. If one organization perceives the "cost" to cooperation in terms of money, time or energy to be greater than the benefits, it will resist it.

- *Goals:* Even if there is consensus on overarching corporate goals, specific joint actions are often perceived to work against the interest of one organization or against another limited goal. The degree to which an entity feels it is flexible to change its current goals, tasks and philosophy to adopt the course of action being proposed will also have an impact.

- *Geography:* To allow another entity to operate in one organization's area is often perceived as an indication that it, alone, is not doing an adequate job. It also may be perceived as a duplication of effort, a source of potential confusion both internally and externally or a lack of control over the "intruding" personnel.

- *Methods:* General agreement on goals alone can still lead to conflict if one party feels the approach proposed to reach goals would be ineffective or counterproductive to other interests of the organization. In addition, one organization may feel a degree of "ownership" over an activity or technique that another organization plans to use.

- *Identity:* Resistance also occurs when an organization feels that proposed cooperation would adversely affect how it is viewed by other entities both inside and outside the company.

- *Personalities:* Key players may be disliked by other stakeholders because they are perceived as representing an organizational or political threat. This can undermine efforts toward collaboration.

Tom VanHootegem, Director of National Accounts at Boise Office Solutions, has implemented a strategy around a "culture of recognition." He credits the following with creating a high level of alignment between the branch offices and the national accounts program.

Best Practice

"Boise uses its voicemail system to quickly communicate important information about national accounts to the community of field sales reps, their managers and NAMs. The early messages were designed to be informational—we were embarrassed one time when a salesperson cold-called one of our newly signed national accounts and heard through the prospect that we already were their supplier. The voicemail messages ensured that information like this was quickly disseminated.

As I was planning those early messages, it made sense to mention the names of the employees who had helped create these successes. Then, as our national accounts program gained momentum and there were more and more of these calls, my boss (who hated voicemail) asked me to limit the calls to once a week.

The next thing you know, we've institutionalized employee recognition! It is amazing how this weekly call, which we call the National Accounts Friday Report, motivates employees. Every week ends with literally hundreds of employees calling in to listen to that voice mail message that might acknowledge their contributions to our national accounts success. I've visited branch offices where new sales reps introduce themselves to me saying, 'Someday you'll be saying my name on your call!' I see branch managers throughout the country pushing their people to be named as contributing to the success of national accounts. Talk about having alignment with your goals!

Now everyone has laptops, and information can be disseminated via e-mail, but I've stayed with voicemail. You can convey emotion through voice that you simply can't via text. You can also have more fun with voice. We've introduced popular game show formats, for example. The calls still include information. When we explain why we lost a deal (which, fortunately, isn't nearly as frequently as the wins), we never include an employee's name, but we do include the reasons our competitor won. We have gained so much buy-in to our national accounts program through these calls.

I depend on my NAMs to submit the information I need for the calls. I carefully script the message based on the information submitted, including:

- The account and the nature of its business;
- The nature of the win (e.g., new account, growth in account, win-back of a previously lost account);
- Dollar value of the win;
- The names of any associates involved in the "win";
- Key factors that contributed to the win; and
- Competitor from whom the business was taken."

Compensation Conflicts

Compensation alignment within SAM programs is the art of selecting performance measures that fit not only the realities of an individual job, but also support cohesion of the team worldwide. Although we do not propose to help you construct your compensation program in this book, recent SAMA research, conducted in partnership with The Alexander Group, sheds light on some key compensation challenges that lead to misalignment and impede the SAM from getting his or her job done. Use this information to challenge your existing compensation models and, hopefully, eliminate some of the elements that reinforce behavior that is counterproductive to your overall customer strategy.

Who Gets Credit?

There are often conflicting opinions regarding who gets credit for global or national account sales. This is handled in multiple ways. Some companies don't allow split crediting. Unfortunately, they get what they pay for. In these companies, global or key account managers are unable to securely focus on selling into remote locations and sales are left for competitors to secure. Other companies decide it is too difficult to proactively determine a crediting approach and default to "let's decide at the end of the year." This results in an internal focus with dysfunctional politics and positioning at the expense of a planned, coordinated sales coverage process. The Alexander Group recommends explicit rules for sales crediting with the following guidelines:

Things to Do:

- *Pay for Persuasion:* Identify the salespeople who share responsibility for persuading a customer versus just generating leads or servicing needs. Limit sales crediting to those who have a "persuasive" role in the sales process.

- *Split Commission for Commission Plans:* If salespeople are on a commission plan, develop and communicate a scheme for splitting commission based on the relative roles of the players. If the global or key account manager negotiates a global contract, but the real persuasion is at the remote locations, a 25 / 75% crediting may be appropriate. This should be communicated ahead of the sales event so all players are aware of the impact of each sale.

- *Double Credit for Bonus Plans:* If salespeople are paid for performance relative to goal, inflate quotas so that all players share in both the accountability for the results as well as the credit for the sale.

"Unfortunately, the compensation plan is not devised in such a way that the guy in France who is covering 'Customer A' benefits by the fact that 'Customer A' has had a good year with us around the world. I really think a portion of their compensation or their bonus should be based on how the account does on a worldwide basis. That would take a person's perspective off the end of their nose and put it at least out at arm's length."

Things to Avoid – Don't:

• *Pay for Service:* Occasionally, due to geographic considerations, a salesperson is assigned accountability for making service calls on an account that buys centrally. Where the opportunity for selling at a remote location is minimal or non-existent, sales crediting is not appropriate.

• *"Print-New-Money" by Over-crediting:* It is important to separate the persuasive sales activities that result in new business from the service activities that are necessary to achieve desired levels of customer satisfaction. It is easy to fall into the trap of succumbing to whining and over-credit.

Rethinking Performance Measures

Many performance measures used in sales compensation plans are old and reliable—units, revenue, margin, growth. According to Scott Sands and Mark Blessington of Sibson Consulting, more meaningful performance measures are required to achieve truly effective global alignment. In a recent article on the subject for *Velocity*™ Magazine, they shared the following principles that sales organizations or even single global account teams can employ:

Push the boundaries with new performance measures. Consider measures such as new product revenue, price realization, account penetration (share), customer retention, acquisition cost, milestone achievement, balanced performance, order linearity, account profitability, etc. The source for performance measure ideas is a deep understanding of the job description of an individual. Get to the heart of the parameters that dictate success or failure for the individual, the team and the company. Rein in this creativity when discussions range too far outside the job's sphere of control.

Interlock performance measures up and down the management hierarchy and across functional relationships. If one job cares about revenue growth and another job cares about profit and both are important to the company and both jobs have to work together frequently, apply both performance measures to each job (in varying percentage weightings to retain focus). For example, most companies put the top sales executive on the executive management incentive plan in addition to the sales compensation plan. This person must operate with one foot in each world and strive for balanced achievement. Global account team personnel are subject to a similar environmental conflict, but are usually eligible for only one (sales) compensation plan. Multiple interlocking performance measures can help with alignment.

Stay with objective measures (quantifiable if possible). Subjective sales compensation measures rarely translate well across geographic and cultural boundaries. Subjective, "catch-all" measures such as MBOs require significant administration effort and are rarely the panacea they were projected to be. If qualitative measures must be used, be sure to add as much structure as possible (grading guidelines, etc.) to ensure consistency.

Stay with three or fewer measures and establish each measure as 20% or more of an individual's total incentive. Focus is important and easily lost.

Bear in mind that compensation plans don't just cause misalignment amongst the rank and file of sales and service organizations. If top executives are measured (and therefore focused) on goals that either clash or do not support the overall customer strategy, conflict will result. According to this SAMA member, his geographically-focused senior executive is not incented to behave in ways that are best for the customer overall:

"I believe that the President of U.S. Corporate Accounts in my company should be held accountable for the revenue generated by his 60 global accounts on a worldwide basis, and not just the U.S. Without that, people think that what happens to their customer outside of their home country will have no impact on the relationship or the success that they have with that customer within their home country. I see that as a very parochial view. I believe this would force the president to put on his global hat and say, 'If we screw this company up in Asia, I may end up losing the business in America.'"

"50% of the sell is internal, and part of the big problem there is compensation. What we're trying to do is change the measurement systems from local P&Ls to measurement of the management team around the world. That is based on service levels, productivity, quality – not just profit – because in the past a particular plant or division could make a profit and not provide a service to a global account and still make their budget, and still make their bonuses. Well, that's ridiculous, so one thing we've instituted now is that 25% of the compensation of branch managers is based on their customer satisfaction ratings for global accounts. That's going to hit them in the pocket and it's going to get their attention, which should help."

Information Infrastructure

"(Our system is) great for marketing people and people who are running businesses. But it's not very useful for account management and sales people who are trying to manage from a customer's perspective."

Effectively capturing, disseminating and leveraging information inside your firm is the lynchpin to serving customers around the world in a coordinated, consistent manner—responding quickly and effectively to changing competitive conditions, and offering products or services to customers more quickly, cheaply, efficiently and innovatively. For this reason, senior sales management must play an active and visible role in the development of systems, processes and people that enable your firm to harness the potential of the intellectual capital you possess. Your focus should be a dual one: provide an information infrastructure that not only supports the efficient delivery of basic customer requirements, but also fosters a knowledge-based environment that enables value creation. Your challenges in doing so will likely fall into two distinct categories: using technology effectively and addressing the cultural issues surrounding collaboration.

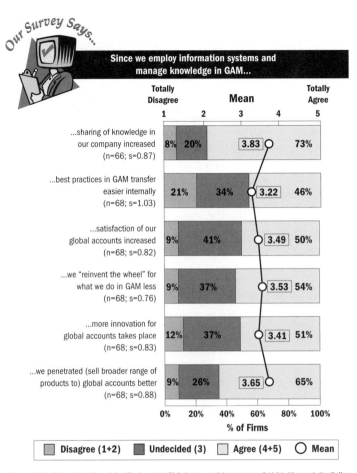

Our Survey Says...

Since we employ information systems and manage knowledge in GAM...

	Totally Disagree		Mean		Totally Agree
	1	2	3	4	5

...sharing of knowledge in our company increased (n=66; s=0.87) — 8% | 20% | 3.83 | 73%

...best practices in GAM transfer easier internally (n=68; s=1.03) — 21% | 34% | 3.22 | 46%

...satisfaction of our global accounts increased (n=68; s=0.82) — 9% | 41% | 3.49 | 50%

...we "reinvent the wheel" for what we do in GAM less (n=68; s=0.76) — 9% | 37% | 3.53 | 54%

...more innovation for global accounts takes place (n=68; s=0.83) — 12% | 37% | 3.41 | 51%

...we penetrated (sell broader range of products to) global accounts better (n=68; s=0.88) — 9% | 26% | 3.65 | 65%

0%   20%   40%   60%   80%   100%

% of Firms

■ Disagree (1+2)   ■ Undecided (3)   □ Agree (4+5)   ○ Mean

Source: 2001, Organizing Knowledge Exchange in Global Account Management, SAMA, Harvard, St. Gallen.

Technology: The #1 Problem

If you are like most companies we've talked to, you are still struggling to understand and utilize technology to enhance and automate SAM processes. For three years running, SAMA research has shown that the *Utilization of CRM Tools* is the weakest competency across SAM programs, garnering a mere 2.4 average rating on a scale of 1 (low) to 5 (high). It's no wonder that technology-related questions are the most frequently posed to SAMA by practitioners.

With recent advances in Web-based applications and infrastructure, the role that technology **can** play in effective SAM has become significant. Yet, the technology component of SAM is misunderstood and under-utilized. A big part of the problem is that many of the prevalent tech solutions are not an especially good fit for strategic account management. According to Rob Desisto, Vice President of the CRM practice at Gartner, "There is an underserved market for customer-facing applications that integrate the customer into the SAM process and provide value directly to them." Companies have evaluated and implemented many types of technology including CRM, portals, collaboration tools and document management systems, but these technologies are too often designed to assist general sales operations and do not provide the necessary functionality for SAM. They are often too complex, too internally focused or designed to provide more of a management reporting tool than a true customer-focused solution for SAM. Consequently, the intended users within SAM programs see little value in the technology because it does not help them do their jobs more efficiently or effectively. The result is that the technology is unused and falls by the wayside, which amounts to an enormous waste of time, effort and money—commodities that companies don't have in surplus these days.

Goal #1: Enhance Operational Efficiency

The first challenge of effective strategic account management that technology should address is operational efficiency. A chief SAM complaint is that there is too much manual work required by existing systems, which is exacerbated by vanishing administrative support. Effectively automating much of the account activity at the tactical level removes the coordination of "low-value activity" from the account manager. Well-executed automation increases response rates and customer satisfaction, lowers cost of sales and allows account managers to spend more time on strategic matters instead of ensuring that "*no one drops the ball.*" Over time, it can even increase the number of accounts that each SAM can effectively manage.

Although nearly every company has implemented sales automation tools, few have achieved true efficiencies as a result, particularly with respect to managing strategic accounts. "Failure to adopt" has been the primary culprit. SAMA research indicates that the lack of flexibility and ease-of-use of such tools, too often dictated by IT organizations, are the primary cause of that failure. Survey respondents complained most about the overall difficulty in implementation and integration with existing systems, from getting these technologies to work with legacy data and existing internal processes, to having to retrain their entire workforce in order to take advantage of new features, to difficulty in getting information from a variety of sources (Web browsers, e-mail, PDAs and smart phones, etc.). Bottom line—for maximum adoption, the tools must provide real value to the account team, making their jobs easier without causing any disruption in the way they work.

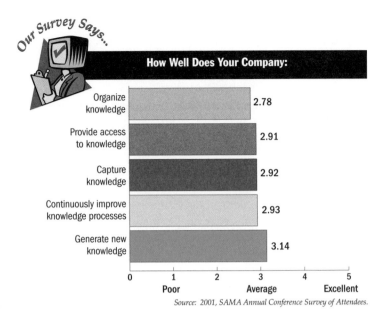

Source: 2001, SAMA Annual Conference Survey of Attendees.

Goal #2: Preserve Institutional Memory

A major issue preventing better performance with strategic accounts is the lack of "institutional memory" for the account. This is the recorded knowledge of the account history, contacts, requirements, issues resolved and not resolved and visibility into other divisions or departments in the account. A good deal of the knowledge that has accumulated in the company may never be discovered or passed along, with much of it susceptible to disappearing when employees leave the firm. Studies done by the Insight Group found that 80% of a strategic relationship lies in "unstructured" information. Unfortunately, this is the critical information that typically never makes it into any of the systems commonly used by companies today. Effective use of technology can be used to create an accessible and permanent memory for all of the activities of an account, helping to reduce the "left hand / right hand" syndrome as well as the frequent finger pointing that occurs immediately after a deliverable is not met for a customer.

Despite the availability of newer and better tools, companies are still finding it difficult to create an effective "audit trail," which hampers their ability to develop effective account plans to drive maximum revenue. The account team at one high-tech manufacturing company told us the situation got so bad that they would routinely need to ask their customer to help them understand what was happening in the account because internally, the left hand had no idea of what the

"One of the things technology does is it takes some of the control, or at least perceived control, of the sales rep away from the rep. Where 'Joe sales rep' managed all that knowledge in his head by just being around the customer, now we've got that in a computer file that is shared by the organization at large. If Joe goes away to the competitor, he may not be able to take that account. He doesn't own all the knowledge anymore."

right hand was doing! Your challenge is to select tools that enable the capture of this type of information in your unique environment and corporate culture.

Goal #3: Facilitate Customer Access

Account penetration and protection are directly related to the customer intimacy that is achieved by account managers. The challenge to increasing customer intimacy is the "wall" that often exists between the supplier and the customer. This wall is created by the natural vendor / customer relationship and the "impedance mismatch" between the vendor's sales cycle and its required activities and the customer's strategic sourcing plan and its required activities. The result is a lack of good communication and visibility between the companies that prevents a stronger relationship. Web-based technologies can now give a customer visibility into the status of issues, deliverables and information needed within the relationship—taking the communication burden off the SAM and creating an almost self-serve (and secure) environment for the customer. These technologies enable customers to more actively engage with account teams. Customers are allowed to provide input into the sales process, control and even assign deliverables, all of which empower them in a way they have never been before.

Best Practice

Dell Corporation facilitated customer access to information when they set up what they termed "Premier Pages" for each major corporate customer. Through a Premier Page, a customer like Shell Corporation could access the Dell account team, check and place orders, get product information and receive notices. Premier Pages is considered a huge success at Dell, as it delivered on three primary objectives: it lowered the cost to service customers because they asked fewer questions to live operators, customers bought more from Dell through the tailored and co-branded site and they were happier due to their ability to immediately access information right when they wanted it. This program has been so successful that today 40% of Dell's entire business flows through Premier Pages! Account managers can use these powerful new technologies as a central exchange of communication, or "virtual SPOC" to increase operational efficiency and coordination, gain global visibility, increase customer intimacy and drive the account plan for greater revenues.

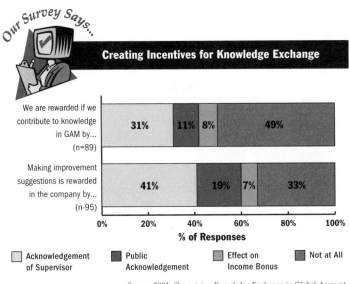

Creating Incentives for Knowledge Exchange

We are rewarded if we
contribute to knowledge
in GAM by...
(n=89)

Making improvement
suggestions is rewarded
in the company by...
(n-95)

% of Responses

- Acknowledgement of Supervisor
- Public Acknowledgement
- Effect on Income Bonus
- Not at All

Source: 2001, Organizing Knowledge Exchange in Global Account Management, SAMA, Harvard, St. Gallen.

Where Do We Go from Here?

It is imperative that executive sales leaders make an explicit connection between their company's competitive strategy and how they use information to support it. SAMA research indicates four key activities to undertake before you bring in technology:

1. *Requirements Definitions:* Goals and metrics must be defined before technologies are brought in. Companies must understand their customers and know where customer relationships are headed. It is a good idea to benchmark with like-minded organizations before beginning the selection process.

2. *Simplicity and Effective Implementation:* Fully map out the implications of implementing technologies in the short and long-term. Companies will achieve greater success by choosing and implementing simpler, proven technologies before choosing more complex ones. Effective implementation plans are the key to success.

3. *Internal / External Collaboration and Management Support:* Multifunctional teams must be brought to bear when specifying, assessing and choosing technologies. Strategic customers should be involved with the development of strategic plans. Early management support is crucial to successful technology selection and implementation.

4. *Training:* Training plans must be created to ensure successful technology implementation and use. Users must be shown that the

"The main issue at the end of the day was the obligation one way or the other to work on it consistently...It's very easy to set them up but the difficulty is in the updating. And that's the reason why it died because it's true that it brought a lot of positive things to us but at the end of the day it was not updated."

value of the new technology outweighs the time required to learn and use it. Implementers must be aware of the need for corporate culture changes to pave the way for effective technology use.

Summary

This chapter was designed to highlight key areas where senior sales management is most needed, and best positioned, to make a difference in the ability of strategic sales teams to positively IMPACT both your most important customers and your own firm. While companies clamor for enough talented people to take on the task of managing complex accounts, remember that even the most outstanding group of professionals cannot rise to the occasion in the face of overwhelming organizational obstacles. In fact, it is your very best who are at risk if they are prevented from achieving their goals by the very same organization that has charged them with driving toward them. Just as they are the chief customer advocate inside your firm, so must you be their advocate where you have the potential to make an IMPACT—and sometimes even where it seems that you don't.

"I am in charge of Enterprise Selling / Interdivisional Partnering at a *Fortune 100* firm with 14 business units and operations in nearly 50 countries. Each business unit operates independently, and some even compete with each other. Additionally, a distribution unit sells its products and also sells competitive products. Of the 3,000 sales reps employed, over half are commission only. Obviously, some are focused on their own business needs and tend to work on the old selling model of pushing product since this is how they are compensated. NAMs are customer-driven, but work for one of the 15 business units.

I accepted this position two years ago, as a corporate overlay to the business units, with a charge to develop ground-level success and the support of a corporate sponsor with some teeth. I was chosen by a group of cross-functional executives, including the SVP of Sales & Marketing, who worked with eight of the business units and shared the objective to satisfy our customers by working together.

To establish the need for the program, I surveyed our top 20 markets and customers. My mandate was created based on their response: 'Your firm is one of the hardest companies to do business with.'

I then equated that statement to dollars. Since each customer was doing over one million dollars with us, the potential for loss was twenty million dollars. My first task was to get the executive office and senior leaders to see that this was starting to hurt. My corporate sponsor recommended a team approach to designing a plan we could implement over time.

We began by asking 3,000 selected sales reps, 'What's the hardest thing that we are facing today?' We discovered that the reps did not even know where to go if they had an inquiry. We went to each business head and asked them to identify one 'go-to' person: A director-level person that would function as traffic cop, and direct an inquiry to the appropriate division.

We made the case to each of the chosen 14 by leveraging the support of our corporate sponsor and positioning this as the next step in their career development; ('Your boss was the one that recommended you for these reasons'). We leveraged information from the survey and some of their top customers in the presentation. For example, one business unit had just lost a major customer and two million dollars in revenue. After analyzing the loss, they determined that if just one of the other business units had been involved, it would have expanded our firm's influence and they would not have lost the revenue.

We also addressed the issue of territorial protectionism and control that was part of the philosophy of each business unit, and communicated what was in it for them. This led to the creation of 14 Business Development Coordinators as part of the team.

We are now in the process of developing tools and resources for the team. This includes a business development database that will track the number of leads that are forwarded. We are also developing an incentive program for all salespeople that will include a finder's fee for business that will come from our corporate budget. Our objectives are tied to the growth expected when accounts targeted for cross-divisional potential register an increase from other businesses. In addition, our company is implementing a supply chain initiative that is a stepping-stone to what the company needs to do to knock down the walls between the business units. This initiative offers significant value since it focuses on 'making it easier to satisfy our customers.'

We have the idea and we have the strategy. Now it's a people issue as we overcome the mindset 'we've always done it this way.'"

Chapter 10:
A Message to the CEO:
Is This YOUR Company?

"I believe that the President of U.S. Corporate Accounts in my company should be held accountable for the revenue generated by his 60 global accounts on a worldwide basis, and not just the U.S. Without that, people think that what happens to their customer outside of their home country will have no impact on the relationship or the success that they have with that customer within their home country. I see that as a very parochial view. I believe this would force the president to put on his global hat and say, 'If we screw this company up in Asia, I may end up losing the business in America.'"

Case Study:
The Opportunity Cost of an Opportunity Lost

The Players:

Multi-billion $ global components supplier
Global account, multi-billion $ major industry force

The Current State:

Supplier has 25% of existing business. Considers Customer strategically important. GAM has good relationship with components buyer. Customer wants to reduce its component supplier base and establish close working relationships with two firms. Supplier is viewed as a technology leader, but has become less cost competitive.

The Opportunity:

Customer has new product developing worth $65M incremental revenue potential over two years. Wants 7% price relief on current business of $20M in exchange for 70-80% of the total component purchases associated with new project. Customer brings opportunity to Supplier in advance of the official RFP process, making it known that Supplier was preferred.

The GAM's Response:

GAM does financial analysis on the $1.3M discount and constructs a business case outlining the benefits of becoming a strategic partner to this Customer, a market powerhouse seeking to consolidate its suppliers. The GAM's goal—provide a comprehensive quote on the new project (50% of the revenue potential) to demonstrate supplier capabilities and use this deal as leverage to win a minimum of 65% of the much larger ($80M) base of business.

The Supplier's Corporate Response:

Supplier's Japan operation verbally agrees to discount; during the deal, however, it reverses its position due to:

1. Pressure to retain original margins to meet its annual internal commitments;

2. Additional components required re-tooling through the capital budget process by a region that had never supplied this Customer, and whose budgets were already over-run due to other problems; and

3. Increased business beyond this deal was going to be realized by a different region.

A significant amount of inter-regional discussion and dissension ensues to no avail. The price relief proposed by the Customer is rejected and the Supplier issues a standard estimate that excludes several quotable parts because they are considered low-margin items.

The Outcome:

The Customer awards less than 25% of the new product deal to the Supplier. Supplier executives hastily intervene, requesting additional time to re-quote for its previously un-bid components. Customer allows the re-bid, but it is ultimately too little too late. The Supplier wins about 35% of its original goal, leaving a substantial amount of the potential revenue for that project on the table. An indeterminate, yet certainly significant amount of future wallet was left to the Supplier's competitors.

The Moral of the Story:

A successful response to a major opportunity required the cooperation of numerous Supplier entities across several global regions. The decision to reject the pre-RFP deal revealed the

Supplier's inability to reconcile its internal issues in order to provide a global response. Moreover, the Supplier's decision to provide a partial quote hurt the GAM's credibility with the Customer. Overall, the Supplier's future position with this Customer is now jeopardized, and although the Customer still views it as a relevant Supplier, it is unlikely to be among the preferred Suppliers as the Customer evolves its supply chain management strategies toward vendor reduction.

Where Are YOU in Your Customers' Strategies?

As CEO, you already know that your customers are your future. You know that their success or failure will have a critical impact on your company. You know that *their* strategy should be driving *your* strategy. You probably spend a lot of time communicating these messages to your board, your shareholders, your executive team, your employees and your financial backers. Yet the example above illustrates an all-too-common scenario that begs the question: *Is this going on in your company?*

If you were nodding your head in recognition of the situation as you read the case, this chapter will help you identify ways to leverage the authority and leadership of the CEO position to not only prevent such missed opportunities in the future, but to create value for customers in a proactive way. If you are convinced that similar conditions don't exist at your firm, consider these facts about the real Supplier represented in the case:

Fact #1: The Supplier has had a solid strategic account management (SAM) program for several years.

Fact #2: The Supplier invests in the development of its people who manage customer relationships.

Fact #3: The SAM strategy has enjoyed a good degree of senior management commitment.

Fact #4: The Supplier is considered a leader and innovator in its industry.

> *Most Important Fact: The CEO did not know about the situation until it was too late.*

The case is a useful illustration of the many disconnects that can exist between the customer-focused strategy all CEOs strive for, and the silo strategies that drive the various working parts of the firm. As your customers continue to narrow their supply base, they are looking for the commitment of, and access to, their supplier's total operation. They want problem-solving and creative thinking about their business. The Supplier in the case example certainly did not demonstrate to the Customer an ability to do any of these things, even though the firm is capable of it, has provided it in the past and has pockets of excellence in the present.

But what about the future? Given current customer pressures and requirements, suppliers will have to rapidly improve their ability to mobilize their entire organization in order to be left standing when "preferred status" is decided upon.

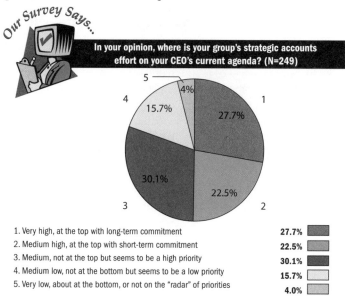

Our Survey Says...

In your opinion, where is your group's strategic accounts effort on your CEO's current agenda? (N=249)

1. Very high, at the top with long-term commitment — **27.7%**
2. Medium high, at the top with short-term commitment — **22.5%**
3. Medium, not at the top but seems to be a high priority — **30.1%**
4. Medium low, not at the bottom but seems to be a low priority — **15.7%**
5. Very low, about at the bottom, or not on the "radar" of priorities — **4.0%**

Source: 2002, SAMA Annual Conference Survey of Attendees.

What Your Front Line Wants You to Know

Imagine the disappointment and frustration of the GAM in the case study. He did a lot of things right. His strong relationship with the Customer was what brought the opportunity to the Supplier in advance of the bid process. He understood the future potential beyond the deal at hand. He developed a business case that supported the deal for the Supplier overall, anticipating some pushback from the region most likely to feel short-changed.

Nobody's perfect, but this GAM was doing many of the things he had been asked to do by both the Customer and by Chief Executives such as yourself. What the GAM didn't have, first and foremost, was the authority to say yes to the deal, nor did he have the backing of someone who carried such authority. Unfortunately, that is not unusual.

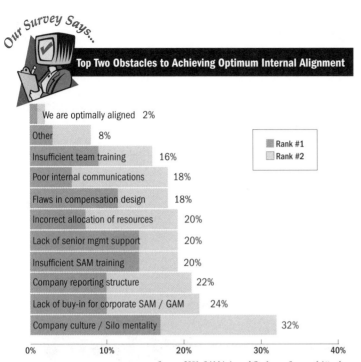

Top Two Obstacles to Achieving Optimum Internal Alignment

We are optimally aligned   2%

Other   8%

| ■ Rank #1 |
| □ Rank #2 |

Insufficient team training   16%

Poor internal communications   18%

Flaws in compensation design   18%

Incorrect allocation of resources   20%

Lack of senior mgmt support   20%

Insufficient SAM training   20%

Company reporting structure   22%

Lack of buy-in for corporate SAM / GAM   24%

Company culture / Silo mentality   32%

0%   10%   20%   30%   40%

Source: 2001, SAMA Annual Conference Survey of Attendees.

This book is designed to teach account managers how to develop a strong internal network that can be mobilized, in the absence of authority, the next time such an opportunity comes around. But building an internal network takes time, and can only go so far to advance the GAM's business case before he comes to an immoveable roadblock. And unless that roadblock is the CEO, then there are things that the CEO can do to ensure that a $125M business opportunity doesn't get left on the table again.

Minimize Conflicting Priorities

According to SAMA research, the single biggest obstacle to alignment is the silo mentality account managers face when trying to implement "total" solutions on behalf of customers. The turf issues that routinely surface in business units, functions and geographies – and in many cases all three simultaneously – are particularly insidious when trying to present one face to the customer. The root of such conflict usually involves perceptions of incompatible goals or threats to relationships. Given the way most matrixed organizations operate, these perceptions are often valid. Deals that are good for the company as a whole are usually not equally beneficial for all the parties involved, and too many firms keep measurement systems in place that fail to compensate the "losers" in a deal. This type of active resistance, which surfaced in the case example, is something that only Executive Management can rectify in terms of "making everyone whole."

The apathy that account managers often encounter can be as dangerous as active resistance. Whereas in the case example there were measures in place that "punished" the Japan branch if it supported the deal, for many the mere lack of *reward* for supporting a customer initiative is enough to place it at a low priority. Where this hurts the customer the most is with service issues. The Executive Suite can either put rewards in place to incent customer-focus across the far reaches of the firm, or take the inverse approach and penalize those who don't comply. In the absence of either, the account manager is spending too much time putting out fires related to inconsistency than he is spending setting strategy with the customer.

Even more powerful is if your sales organization can leverage the power of the Executive Suite on an ongoing basis instead of utilizing it only in dramatic situations with gigantic stakes and a high profile. Consider this example from Siemens:

Best Practice

"I have five bosses in my position as Senior Vice President and Managing Director at Siemens. I report to one of six Board members on the Central Board, and to four Business Unit CEOs who fund the Key Accounts program. The program was created to exploit the power of the Siemens brand. Before the key accounts program was initiated, each group would go independently to a company without understanding what other groups were doing. This created conflict in the mind of the customer and led to decreased productivity and missed opportunities.

My team of 30 KAMs directs all the people in operations worldwide that handle the account. They have no authority to set plans, incent or hire and fire. What they **do** have is a charter from the Chairman of the Board that says they are responsible for worldwide strategy, planning and leadership of the customer. Everyone knows that each KAM reports through me to the Board; it was set up this way so people would recognize that the KAM is 'close to God.' The response to the program has also created an informal charter from the customer, who now demands 'one team' from Siemens."

Play a Visible Role

When there are conflicting agendas, the existing systems and policies are not always enough to prevent a stalemate in terms of handling a customer issue. It can take the sweeping authority of the CEO to remove certain obstacles. The key here is to adopt a formal escalation process to respond quickly, decisively and proactively in situations such as the one posed in the opening case. The CEO who plays an active and visible role supporting the efforts of the SAM team makes a powerful statement to those employees who are less likely to feel a sense of ownership or accountability towards the customer. When the organization knows that this is your stance, they will also be more likely to behave in a way that your intervention is not required.

Perhaps the greatest role the CEO can play is direct contact with the customer itself. A SAM can be more effective at selling to the executive level with the participation of his or her own executives, especially when they find themselves politically blocked by someone in the customer's organization. Moreover, when the Executive Suite is used in a focused way with strategic customers, it typically generates increased customer commitment and strategic-level conversations.

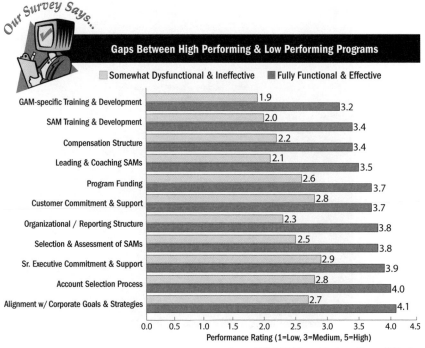

Our Survey Says...

Gaps Between High Performing & Low Performing Programs

☐ Somewhat Dysfunctional & Ineffective   ■ Fully Functional & Effective

Category	Somewhat Dysfunctional & Ineffective	Fully Functional & Effective
GAM-specific Training & Development	1.9	3.2
SAM Training & Development	2.0	3.4
Compensation Structure	2.2	3.4
Leading & Coaching SAMs	2.1	3.5
Program Funding	2.6	3.7
Customer Commitment & Support	2.8	3.7
Organizational / Reporting Structure	2.3	3.8
Selection & Assessment of SAMs	2.5	3.8
Sr. Executive Commitment & Support	2.9	3.9
Account Selection Process	2.8	4.0
Alignment w/ Corporate Goals & Strategies	2.7	4.1

Performance Rating (1=Low, 3=Medium, 5=High)

Source: 2002, SAMA Annual Conference Survey of Attendees.

Invest in Customer Innovation Like You Do In Product Innovation

Most large companies spend huge sums on product R&D without any certainty as to which part of that R&D will turn into revenue and when. By contrast, many SAM programs are prevented from receiving the funding they need, often because they are held to impossibly high standards of certainty about their payback potential. CEOs should reconsider their investment strategies in customer innovation, or they could face a painful scenario like this one:

"I was hired by the CEO of a $500 million division of a $19 billion company to build a strategic accounts program, aimed at creating $100 million client relationships within two years. All the right words were spoken and we had agreement on an 18-month game plan to position us solidly within qualified global targets. Eleven months into it, I can point to two of these targets (from a team of six strategic account managers) where senior relationship development has led to qualified opportunities with $100 million plus potential. At least two of the other four SAMs have the potential to move into this ballpark within the next six to 12 months. However, with current high pressure on all parts of the business, the CEO has decided he needs 'soccer players, not croquet players' to bring in immediate results, regardless of contract size. He questions whether the SAMs can make the transition. The SBU leaders are focused entirely on meeting their own P&L targets, resulting in minimal cross-SBU cooperation. Even worse, the current environment has caused a 'hunkering down' that means little to no 'out of the box' thinking—an absolute necessity for getting to first base on opportunities of $100 million magnitude. Meanwhile, the division is now for sale. My SAMs are all looking for new positions outside the company. So am I. With the benefit of this experience, here's what I'll do next time:

• Validate the CEO's ability to stick with a plan when the going gets tough. I'll want to see a track record;

• Get evidence that SBU leaders and the CEO are all on the same page and committed to a unified success; and

• Make sure there's a 'change of control' clause and a reasonable severance commitment in the contracts of my people."

Strategic Accounts Leader

Your Mandate

The CEO is by nature concerned with all facets of the firm he or she runs, not one particular division or function or geography. Most of them are keenly aware of the inefficiencies inside their own organization in terms of identifying and acting on new ways of doing business. A perfect example of this is the following comment from Edward M. Kopko, Chairman, CEO and President of Butler International, a $450 million provider of technical and technology services. During a CEO roundtable sponsored by Chief Executive Magazine, Kopko struck at the heart of this issue in a most compelling way:

"The biggest obstacle to successful outsourcing is our own organizations. As CEO, I don't spend enough time with our suppliers to hear their ideas about outsourcing opportunities. The issue of empires is an obstacle to the whole concept of outsourcing. I know people in my own company will think, 'I don't want to even go near those areas, because you're talking about blowing up my empire.' I don't know what we can do to help break down that kind of wall, because we're all so busy we don't have enough time to say, 'I'm going to listen to all my suppliers' ideas every year.' I have to delegate that, and then as soon as I've delegated it, I've built the wall that I'm afraid of."

As CEO, there's good news all around in our message to you. First, you have the authority to have an immediate IMPACT on the financial position of your firm by removing just some the obstacles that stand in the way of your sales organization optimizing customer relationships.

Second, you have a legion of dedicated people at the customer interface who will jump at the chance to maximize your participation.

And finally, there is distinct competitive advantage that will accrue to firms who can align better around their customers. If you make known your willingness to learn about your firm's pain points and opportunities in this area, there is likely to be a flood of information that comes your way. Alternatively, ask yourself these questions as you begin to examine the ways you can help your firm have more IMPACT on your customers.

Voice of the Customer

· *Are you able to evaluate how easy (or difficult) your company is to work with?*

· *Do you see things through your customers' eyes?*

· *Do you talk with customers, meet with them and listen to their issues and objectives?*

· *How well do you understand the future needs of your company's key customers?*

Executive Team

· *How do you use customer needs and feedback to drive your company's strategy?*

· *What expectations do you have of your leadership team to interface with key accounts?*

· *Have you established "stakeholders" at the senior executive level for key accounts?*

· *Are your senior executives measured and compensated on their participation in the SAM program?*

· *To what extent do you require your leaders to support cross-entity initiatives, versus only their own silos?*

Resource Allocation

· *Have you communicated your commitment to the SAM program? How?*

· *Are there processes in place that will facilitate employees working across silos?*

· *Have you explicitly communicated how entities that give something up for the good of the corporation will be protected?*

Functional Expertise

· *Are employees within the silos granted the time to contribute their expertise to broader initiatives?*

Author Biographies

Jane Helsing is Vice President, Strategic Accounts for Personnel Decisions International. She works with a variety of companies to strengthen salespeople's ability to create committed customers. The processes that Ms. Helsing introduces to her customers have proven results in such areas as customer feedback and measurement, account team effectiveness and strategic account program effectiveness.

Her responsibilities include consulting with clients—implementing both standard and customized tools that will help employees manage and assess the quality of relationships with their customers, suppliers and work teams. As lead for PDI's strategic account management practice area, she has both created new processes and helped to customize PDI's core offerings for the SAM function. She also manages licensee relationships through which PDI extends its global reach. Ms. Helsing speaks at a variety of industry conferences in the U.S., Canada and Europe.

Ms. Helsing's PDI employment began in 1992 with QI International, a company then acquired by PDI in 1998. Prior to 1992 she spent her career at AT&T in a variety of consumer-industry related positions.

Ms. Helsing has served on SAMA's Board of Directors since 1995 and was its president in 1997. She serves as a mentor to undergraduate sales majors at the College of St. Catherine in St. Paul, Minnesota. She earned her M.S. in Statistics from Rutgers University, New Brunswick, New Jersey and her B.A. in Mathematics from Susquehanna University, Selinsgrove, Pennsylvania.

About Personnel Decisions International (PDI)

"Maximize Potential · Accelerate Success"

PDI helps organizations worldwide improve their performance and achieve strategic results through people. They partner with their clients to:

- Understand the talent implications of their strategies;
- Design and implement solutions that improve individual leadership and organizational performance; and
- Accelerate change and drive lasting improvement throughout the organization.

Specific areas of expertise help clients:

- Improve talent decisions by accurately measuring performance readiness and potential;
- Develop strategy, utilizing information collected through "voice of the customer" feedback systems;
- Enhance sales effectiveness, including people development and implementation of strategic account management programs;
- Recognize and retain top talent, through the design or enhancing of talent management systems;
- Ensure they can execute their business strategies, by defining the performance and capabilities required; and
- Develop leadership capabilities.

PDI's products and services also include one-on-one coaching, 360-degree feedback processes, training and development workshops, employee and customer surveys, competency models and customized approaches for needs related to talent development.

Headquartered in Minneapolis, Minnesota, PDI serves its clients through 29 full-service operating offices throughout the United States, Europe, Asia and Australia. PDI also has strategic alliances with several established consulting organizations in Europe and Latin America.

PDI's services and products are based on extensive research and more than 30 years of experience in working with organizations around the world.

For more information, contact PDI client relations at 920-997-6995 (in the U.S. 800-633-4410) or visit PDI's Web site at www.personneldecisions.com.

· S ·

Barbara Geraghty is the author of *Visionary Selling*, published by Simon & Schuster in 1998. She speaks at national sales meetings, worldwide sales meetings and association conventions to 25,000 people or more annually. Clients include Eli Lilly, SAP, Rockwell, PeopleSoft and Siemens.

Throughout a decade of exceptional sales performance, Barbara set sales records in every position from telemarketing to regional sales manager. Before founding her own firm, she was the #1 sales manager in the Pacific Division of Sprint.

Barbara is also the author of *Secrets of Peak Performers*, based on interviews with top business leaders and CEOs. She received her Bachelor of Arts, Communications from California State University, Fullerton, is a member of National Speakers Association and is included in Who's Who of American Women. She has been featured in articles in Selling Power, Entrepreneur magazine and on CNBC.

About Visionary Selling

Visionary Selling teaches salespeople the business acumen and financial competency to articulate high-level value propositions to executives.

It provides the following training and tools:

- *Visionary Selling*, published by Simon & Schuster;

- Keynote presentations by Barbara Geraghty, author of *Visionary Selling;*

- Sales Training;

- e-Learning products for web-based training using your intranet or computer-based training on CD-ROM; and

- Distance Learning options for follow-up, including teleconferencing and webinars.

Barbara Geraghty provides keynote presentations, sales training and e-Learning courses to companies interested in increasing their competency in selling to executives. Average ROI is $32 for every $1 invested in Visionary Selling training. Visit www.visionaryselling.com or call 800-590-4332.

Visionary Selling may be purchased at www.amazon.com.

Opportunities

Are you interested in becoming a distributor of Visionary Selling programs and products? We have opportunities available for exceptional salespeople who are currently selling and/or delivering sales training programs. Please complete the Contact Us form from the Visionary Selling Home Page. In the box marked "How did you hear about us?" type Distributor Opportunity.

<u>Client List</u>

Adaptec

Alcatel

American Management Association

Arthur Andersen

AT&T

Attachmate

Braun Consulting

Cabletron

Carlson Marketing Group

Ceridian

CIGNA

Computer Associates

Dell Computer

Eli Lilly

Exide

Experian

Ingram Micro

Johnson Controls

Keane

Key Bank

Kingston Technology

Lucent Technologies

Northwestern Mutual

Paine Weber

PeopleSoft

Rockwell Automation
  & Rockwell Software

Sales & Marketing Executives
  International

SAP America

Scantron

Siemens

Silicon Graphics

Sterling Software

Strategic Account Management
  Association

Sybase

Symantec

Telecordia

United States Postal Service

Xerox

• ∫ •

Lisa Napolitano joined the Strategic Account Management Association (SAMA) in 1991 as Executive Director charged with revitalizing the organization, which was founded in 1964. Napolitano serves as chief spokesperson for SAMA, an international, non-profit organization with 2500 practitioner members, and the leading information provider on the subject of strategic customer-supplier partnering. Her primary role is to enable SAMA to increase the body of knowledge on the complexities of enterprise relationship management, and to disseminate best practices and research data to business leaders around the world.

Toward this end, Napolitano has guided a robust research agenda that includes studies in areas such as: Account Management Execution; Competencies that Drive Strategic Account Growth; Knowledge Management Practices within Global Customer Teams; Frameworks for Compensating Strategic Account Managers; Best Practices in Global Customer Management; Competency Models for Strategic Account Management Positions; Performance Improvement and Innovation within SAM Programs.

Napolitano has been Editor and contributing author to several books including *Harnessing Global Potential: Insights into Managing Customers Worldwide* (2001), *The Trust Imperative: The Competitive Advantage of Trust-Based Business Relationships* (1998), and *Unlocking Profits: The Strategic Advantage of Key Account Management* (1997). She also serves as Publisher of *Velocity*™, SAMA's Quarterly Magazine, and several other publications such as *Focus: Europe*™, *Focus: Teams*™ and *Focus: Account Manager*™.

A frequent speaker on strategic customer management issues, Napolitano has presented at conferences in North America and Europe, and has addressed numerous corporate sales teams.

Napolitano serves on the Board of Directors of SAMA, as well as the Russ Berrie Institute for Professional Sales. She holds a B.A. in Politics from Princeton University, and an Honorary Doctorate in Business Administration from Southampton Institute.

About SAMA

Founded in 1964 and with over 2,800 current members worldwide, SAMA attracts the strategic customer management profession's most influential decision-makers. Over the past 40 years, the association has earned the reputation of being the SAM profession's knowledge leader, providing members with the high quality resources, training and networking opportunities needed to succeed.

SAMA Mission Statement

The Strategic Account Management Association is a non-profit organization devoted to developing and promoting the concept of customer-supplier collaboration. SAMA is dedicated to the professional development of the individuals involved in the process of managing national, global and strategic customer relationships, and to enabling firms to create greater customer value and achieve competitive advantage accordingly.

SAMA Benefits & Services

Knowledge Resources

To provide members with the high quality and leading information they need, the SAMA Member Services department is constantly scanning the business environment and making relevant information available to members. The association's Online Library is available 24 hours a day, containing nearly 2000 white papers, session presentations, research reports, Web links, case studies, speakers, trainers, consultants and articles specific to strategic account management. How do we maintain this vast Knowledge Network? By being connected to the experts in academia, consulting and research—and by being privy to the opinions and practices of thousands of professional practitioners.

SAMA Publications:

Books:

Impact Without Authority: How to Leverage Internal Resources to Create Customer Value

Harnessing Global Potential: Insights Into Managing Customers Worldwide

The Trust Imperative: The Competitive Advantage of Trust-Based Business Relationships

Unlocking Profits: The Strategic Advantage of Key Account Management

Magazines / Newsletters:

Velocity™

Focus: Account Manager

Focus: Europe

Focus: Teams

Research Reports:

Annual Compensation Study

Global Account Management

Organizing Knowledge Exchange in
Global Account Management

Leading Edge Practices for Measuring and
Managing Customer Loyalty

Strategic Account Management: Benefits,
Critical Factors & Challenges

Education and Training

SAMA's educational events provide Strategic Account
Management professionals with the focused training required to
remain competitive in today's global marketplace. New courses
are introduced on an annual basis and materials are constantly
updated and customized to meet the unique needs of its audience.
The hallmark of SAMA's education and training is the delivery of
practical information that you can use immediately to nurture and
strengthen your most valuable customer relationships.

SAMA Meetings:

<u>Annual Conference:</u> The only event of its kind, enabling you to
customize your curriculum based on your company's development
as well as your personal training goals.

<u>Pan-European Conference:</u> The Pan-European Conference offers
the perspectives of leading practitioners and thinkers on building
an integrated view of the total customer relationship across
products and geographies within an organization.

<u>Annual Executive Leadership Symposium:</u> The Symposium offers
relevant best practice knowledge to the senior executives who lead
their SAM efforts.

<u>Workshops:</u> Skill building workshops provide an interactive
learning experience as well as access to some of the profession's
most respected trainers and consultants.

<u>Best Practice Forums:</u> These forums offer a unique and convenient
venue for practitioners to come together for learning and
networking. The format of these events is informal, with prepared
presentations used as a platform for group discussion and the
sharing of ideas between participants.

Peer Networking

SAMA promotes, inspires and engineers the free exchange of
ideas, insight and knowledge among professionals interested in
strategic customer management. At SAMA, we take networking
seriously because we know the value of connecting with people
who have practical and useful information. In today's hectic world,
we don't take it for granted that such knowledge exchange will

happen naturally—we help you leverage the collective intelligence of our membership by creating opportunities to network with peers that are numerous, varied and convenient. Our educational events enable face-to-face interaction that frequently leads to long-term relationships amongst peers. On a virtual basis, we connect people through e-mail based Special Interest Groups and our Peer Networking Directory of experts in 36 subjects. Our extensive online database features an exclusive network of practitioners, academics and consultants who can bring their insights into your company for truly customized learning. Underlying it all is a SAMA team of Information Specialists who are ready to access our network for you just for the asking.

SAMA Members cover every imaginable industry and a variety of job functions such as:

Director / VP of Strategic Accounts
Director / VP of Sales
Director / VP of Marketing
Director / VP of Business Development
National / Strategic / Global Account Managers
Cross-Functional Team Members
Corporate Sales Training Executives
Consultants
Academics

Contributing Author:

David Peterson, Ph.D., is a Senior Vice President at Personnel Decisions International. He specializes in executive coaching and consulting to help business leaders accelerate learning and improve performance for themselves, their teams and their organizations.

Mr. Peterson is the author of two best-selling books that provide practical advice to help people develop themselves and coach others: *Development FIRST: Strategies for Self-Development* (1995) and *Leader As Coach: Strategies for Coaching and Developing Others* (1996). An expert on coaching, leadership development and managerial effectiveness, Mr. Peterson has been quoted in *Wall Street Journal, Fortune, Time* and *USA Today*.

He received his Ph.D. from the University of Minnesota, specializing in both Industrial/Organizational and Counseling Psychology. He joined PDI in 1985 and has been practice leader for PDI's worldwide coaching services since 1990.